"Trevecca has written a compelling, yet winsome invitation for parents of all ages and stages to 're-member' the significance of our stories in building bridges and planting the seeds of faith. She provides honest, sometimes messy and painful stories from ordinary people like you and me as a way of reminding us of the importance of being authentic and intentional about our traditions, rituals, and storytelling by embracing celebratory moments as well as those involving grief and failure. Chock-full of practicable suggestions on how the church can become family for one another, this timely book is both comforting and challenging."

—**Leslie F. Thyberg**, Trinity School for Ministry, member of ACNA's Committee for Catechesis

The Grandparenting Effect

"Let's get 'RE&AL' about grandparenting is the mantra of *The Grandparenting Effect*: 'Relationally Engaged' and 'Always Listening'! Well-documented research, thoughtful advice, engaging stories from a wide variety of grandparenting situations, helpful chapter summaries, ideas for grandchildren from toddlers to adults—plus prayers and bridge stories as well as timely help for conversations with grandchildren about race and cultural differences—this is an insightful and practical book for grandparents (volunteers, too!), pastors, and church educators to bridge the generational gap with wisdom and joy!"

—**Robbie F. Castleman**, author of *Parenting in the Pew*

"The most influential member of my extended family was my mom. Her influence lives on in her thirteen grandchildren, eleven great-grandchildren, and two great-great grandchildren. Every time the family is together, stories about how Grandma influenced our lives fly around the room. This wide influence was born from, and is carried in, stories. In *The Grandparenting Effect* Trevecca Okholm gives vision for cherishing, cultivating, and appropriating family stories. Marinated in the wisdom of real life, it is both enlightening and encouraging!"

—**Todd Hunter**, Bishop, Churches for the Sake of Others

"Full of memory and meaning, Okholm offers an alternative paradigm for those who care for children and desire to help them build bridges between faith and the culture we live in. Well-researched with contemporary studies, *The Grand-parenting Effect* is chock-full of ideas, prayers, Scripture, and stories that are both heart-warming and heart-breaking. This book will benefit Christian educators, parents, and grandparents (and the children they love) for years to come."

—**Sharon Ely Pearson**, grandmother, Episcopal Christian educator, and author of *Call on Me: A Prayer Book for Young People*

"Professor Okholm describes, in practical, inspirational, and often humorous ways, grandchild activities that do far more than entertain—they result in moments that matter. As a grandparent of twelve myself, I have come away with a desire to create more occasions where the grandchild is invited into what the author calls 'sacred space' and 'holy time.' This is a book that reminds us, delightfully, of what matters most in life. I highly recommend it."

—**Robert L. Millet**, Professor Emeritus of Religious Education, Brigham Young University

"My role as founder of Legacy Coalition forces me to stay up to date on current resources on Christian grandparenting. Trevecca Okholm's new book, *The Grandparenting Effect*, is simply one of the best I have read. It is wonderfully balanced with personal stories, prayers, practical suggestions, and new insights. I learned a lot in reading it, and I will be a better grandfather because of it. I give it my highest recommendation!"

—**Larry Fowler**, founder of The Legacy Coalition

"Being a grandparent just may be your greatest legacy. I read this book through the grid of being a grandparent and I loved it. I have read other grandparenting books and this one comes from a unique and refreshingly different angle. I loved the stories of others and the insight on each page. I've already started using some of the principles I learned with my own grandchildren."

—**Jim Burns**, President, HomeWord, and author of *Doing Life With Your Adult Children*

"Trevecca Okholm knows firsthand the joys and privileges of being a grandparent, and it's evident throughout this book. Filled with countless helpful, encouraging anecdotes, Trevecca's research enriches this volume by including historical and contemporary prayers, spiritual practices from a range of faith traditions, and activities for grandparents to do with their grands of various ages. Now that my eight grandchildren are older, this book will be very helpful with my two great grands. Relationships between generations of the faith family will be deepened by Okholm's work."

—**Scottie May**, Associate Professor Emerita, Wheaton College

"Trevecca Okholm has a long history of serving the church and the academy. In *The Grandparenting Effect*, she shares what she has learned through years of study and her experiences as a grandmother. Written in a very personal and conversational style, Okholm encourages us to take an active role in the faith life of our grandchildren, gives concrete suggestions, and shares inspirational examples of people who have done it well."

—**Robert J. Keeley**, Professor of Education, Calvin University

The Grandparenting Effect

Bridging Generations One Story at a Time

Trevecca Okholm

CASCADE *Books* • Eugene, Oregon

THE GRANDPARENTING EFFECT
Bridging Generations One Story at a Time

Copyright © 2020 Trevecca Okholm. All rights reserved. Except for brief quotations in critical publications or reviews, no part of this book may be reproduced in any manner without prior written permission from the publisher. Write: Permissions, Wipf and Stock Publishers, 199 W. 8th Ave., Suite 3, Eugene, OR 97401.

Cascade Books
An Imprint of Wipf and Stock Publishers
199 W. 8th Ave., Suite 3
Eugene, OR 97401

www.wipfandstock.com

PAPERBACK ISBN: 978-1-7252-5484-8
HARDCOVER ISBN: 978-1-7252-5485-5
EBOOK ISBN: 978-1-7252-5486-2

Cataloguing-in-Publication data:

Names: Okholm, Trevecca, author.

Title: The grandparenting effect : bridging generations one story at a time / by Trevecca Okholm.

Description: Eugene, OR: Cascade Books, 2020 | Includes bibliographical references.

Identifiers: ISBN 978-1-7252-5484-8 (paperback) | ISBN 978-1-7252-5485-5 (hardcover) | ISBN 978-1-7252-5486-2 (ebook)

Subjects: LCSH: Intergenerational communication—Religious aspects—Christianity. | Intergenerational relations—Religious aspects—Christianity. | Christian education of children.

Classification: BV1475.3 .O40 2020 (print) | BV1475.3 (ebook)

Manufactured in the U.S.A.   07/27/20

Dedicated To

Clara Woods Ganzer, the one who set me on
this adventure of grandparenting

And

Elanor Wren Ganzer, the one who came second but
quickly made up for lost time

Two delightful young women who have changed my world,
my values, my future and given me the gifts of joy and hope

And to their "Pops"—my partner in this
grandparenting adventure

Contents

Acknowledgments | ix
Introduction: Sharing Our Stories | xi

Chapter 1: Re-membering Our Place in the Story | 1
    Bridge 1: Stories of Connection | 10

Chapter 2: Building Bridges, Planting Seeds | 17
    Bridge 2: Disconnected Stories | 36

Chapter 3: Refocusing Our Priorities
    (or How *Not* to Be a Consumer Grandparent) | 50
    Bridge 3: Relational Consumption | 61

Chapter 4: Creating Meaning and Moments of R.E.&A.L. | 66
    Bridge 4: Stories of Becoming R.E.&A.L. | 78

Chapter 5: Invitations to Go Further Up and Further In | 90
    Bridge 5: Stories of Redemption | 106

Chapter 6: Naming Sacred Spaces and Holy Time | 129
    Bridge 6: Stories of Sacred Space | 142

Chapter 7: Marking Trails for Those Who Come Behind Us | 147
    Bridge 7: Stories of Paying Attention | 155

Chapter 8: The Grandparenting Effect on Non-Biological
    Grandchildren in Our Lives | 161
    Bridge 8: Stories of Becoming Family for One Another | 175

Appendix | 185
Bibliography | 191

Acknowledgments

I acknowledge my husband, Dennis, my partner in this grandparenting adventure because without his influence and partnership I most likely would never have thought to write this book. To his granddaughters he is known as "Pops" and I as "MeMe." Before he was Pops to Clara and Elanor, he was dad to Ryan and Emily (and father-in-law to Keith), and for hundreds of non-biological children and grandchildren at Wheaton College, Azusa Pacific University, and Fuller Seminary (among other venues) he is affectionately known as "DocOk." For forty-six years and counting we have encouraged and inspired one another and I am thankful to God for bringing us together in this adventure of a lifetime called marriage, parenthood, and grandparenthood.

I also acknowledge my children, Ryan and Emily, and Emily's husband, Keith, for their encouragement and inspiration for much of what has gone into this book! (Not the least of which is giving me grandchildren.)

I am also thankful for all the friends and serendipitous acquaintances who have been willing to share their stories of grandparenting with the readers of this book: Sally Alvino; Susan Ballard; Jennifer Boles; Jennifer Buck; Phyllis Bratton; Kriste Bustamante; David Carlson; Robbie Castleman; Margaret "Toedy" Gray; Mary Kauffman; Ivan Klaussen; Ruth Lampe; Paul Martin; Carol Mermis; Emma O'Brien; Nancy Pearson; Kimberly Phillips; Alix Riley; Marcia Stroup; and Robin Turner. The life lessons I have learned while reading their stories has been inspiring and humbling and I am so blessed to call them all my friends and fellow grandparents on the journey.

Introduction: Sharing our Stories

*From the time you were very little,
you've had people who have smiled you into smiling,
people who have talked you into talking,
sung you into singing, loved you into loving.
So, on this extra special day, let's take some time to
think of those extra special people.
Some of them may be right here, some may be far away.
Some may even be in heaven.
No matter where they are, deep down you know
they've always wanted what was best for you.
They've always cared about you beyond measure and
have encouraged you to be true to the best within you.
Let's just take a minute of silence to think about those people now.*

—Fred Rogers—*commencement address, Westminster Choir College, 1999*

For whom this book has been written

I need to clear something up right from the start. This is a book for grandparents; however, it is *also* a book for the children of grandparents (aka the parents of our grandchildren) who, just like us, are trying to do the very best job possible in raising children/grandchildren with the tools to survive the swiftly changing currents of culture in our twenty-first-century context.

I have also written this book for church leaders seeking to do the very best ministry with families and looking for meaningful ways to bring the generations together in a common sense of belonging to one another and caring for one another.

I have written this book, also, for those who are not yet biological grandparents but hope to be one day. And, as you will discover in the final chapter, I wrote this book to address the privilege we all have of becoming *grandparents* to non-biological children in our communities. Therefore, it is my desire that the reading of this book will not be limited to *just us ordinary grandparents*.

To all you *extraordinarily ordinary grandparents*: I suspect you have spent a few years of your life—some less than others—being single. Then there were probably all those years you spent navigating the waters of marriage, trying to maneuver through some whitewater and maybe even getting capsized a couple of times! Along the journey there came the challenges of navigating and maneuvering the swift flowing rivers of parenthood. And now? If you are reading this book, then it may be that congratulations are in order. You have finally arrived at grandparenthood, and perhaps a few of you have already arrived at *great*-grandparenthood. Only you've arrived to discover that the sandy shoreline of what you've always imagined grandparenting to be has been shifting in our Western culture. That is not a bad thing; in fact, I hope you might agree with me that right now is a pretty exciting time to negotiate the changing sands of grandparenting.

My story of becoming an extraordinarily ordinary grandparent

My husband and I have a good friend who, at last count, has fifteen grandchildren. When asked about having so many grandchildren, Bob smiles and says, *next time I am going to have grandchildren first!*

And, like every grandparent I know, it was with great anticipation that my husband and I waited nine long months from the first announcement that we were having a grandchild until our daughter finally gave birth. Also, like many grandparents I know—including my friend quoted above—I want a *do-over*. By the time we've arrived at grandparent status, some of us wish we'd known as much as we think we know now—and perhaps like me, you wish you had been more intentional when raising your own kids.

Evidently, with the birth of our first grandchild and then our second, our daughter and son-in-law added a new tradition to our family story, the tradition of waiting until the child is actually born before announcing the name. Our daughter and son-in-law had no issue with announcing the gender—very helpful for baby gifting; however, the name—or even discussions around what the name might be—was not ours to know until that new little person came into this world.

We had ideas of what we thought they should name her. Flower names were popular at that time so we thought perhaps Lily or Rose might be name contenders—those would be precious names to call this new little human in our lives.

I flew to Vancouver before the due date—which, typically with a first baby, was many days earlier than the actual date of birth. Then after all day in labor—first at home with a birthing pool, doula, and midwife, the hard decision had to be made—a decision much to our daughter's chagrin—to move the birth to the hospital due to minor complications. In the wee hours of morning on October 31, 2010, Clara arrived. The name was Clara. *Her* name was Clara. My daughter and son-in-law, who apparently both have more wisdom than I, decided to name her after my mother—her great grandmother—who, if she had lived, would have been one hundred barely a month before baby Clara arrived (it would have been even closer if this new little girl had decided to arrive on her due date).

This matters to me. My mother had a hardscrabble life and died of cancer at the age of eighty-two. Because my mother and father married late in life, they didn't give birth to me until my mother was forty-one. And because my husband and I had our children later also, our kids were only nine and twelve when their "Grammie" died. They hardly had time to get to know her before she was gone; however, that first Clara left a legacy of strength and character in their lives, so much so that our daughter and son-in-law decided to name their first child in her memory. Now Clara, our first grandchild, has that legacy to live into—a legacy from a woman she never knew, but who will forever be in her life and memory. And, oh, the stories we get to share with her as she grows up!

Everyone loves a story. This book is filled with them. Stories of our biblical grandparents and stories Jesus told in parables. Some familiar stories have the gift of taking on renewed meaning in our lives as we grow and change, such as stories written by friends and a couple of serendipitous strangers who have, in the moments of meeting, been willing to share their stories with me, thus becoming no longer strangers but new friends. These real stories of ordinary grandparents and grandchildren are provided as *bridges* between each chapter and share accounts of grandparenting successes or grandparenting laments.

And during the writing of this book I had other stories shared with me, such as a story from a granddaughter about the nurture given by her grandfather, and another about a bedridden grandmother who gave a lasting gift of support and influence in the life and career of her granddaughter as she was attending graduate school. Still another heart-wrenching story is from a grandmother in prison who laments her life trajectory and the opportunities she is missing in the lives of her children and grandchildren. And there is a story about the gift of music bringing generations together and still another from the perspective of *faith* grandparents who took college students under their wings and into their homes and made an impact for change in many lives over the years. The stories go on, as you will see as you thumb through the pages of this little book.

I am humbled by those who volunteered to share their stories with me and with you, the readers of this book. I am thankful to each one for the gift and trust they have given me—and given you.

I have long believed in the value of story in our lives and in our faith, so in the process of writing this book, when I came across a story that Jerome Berryman (founder of the Godly Play® foundation) told in his little book *Stories of God at Home*, my conviction of the power of stories was reinforced. He writes about family members who become like "neighboring islands" when they do not share the stories that have the power to connect bridges between their islands:

> I worked at Houston Child Guidance Center from 1983 to 1985 as part of an interdisciplinary team that cared for suicidal children and their families. The team included a psychiatrist, a psychologist, a social worker, a medical doctor, drug expert, and myself, an Episcopal priest. We provided family systems therapy and studied what had gone wrong in the relationships that resulted in children trying to kill themselves. What these families had in common was that they did not tell stories. They did not tell stories about vacations, funny things that happened, sad things, grandparents, births, deaths, pets, hopes, trips, dreams, or any other tales I took for granted, since I had come from a storytelling family. Their communication was reduced to commands, demands, exclamations, brief explanations, and questions requiring short, factual answers. The family members were like neighboring islands without any bridges. There was no narrative to connect

INTRODUCTION: SHARING OUR STORIES

them. What was the treatment? We set up ways to encourage them to tell stories face-to-face.

Because the busyness of our lives and our pragmatic tendencies demand something practical, along with these stories the content of this book also includes practical applications, prayers, blessings, and *ideas to try on*. You will find these included in the *bridges* between chapters. This is added not only to enrich, encourage, and equip grandparents reading this book, but also to create tools that church leaders might integrate into their ministry plans when considering how the generations might be *re-membered* to one another in your faith community.

Additionally, I felt the call to write this book because of the twenty-five plus years I have spent facilitating children and family ministry in the church. Over the years I have had countless conversations with parents, grandparents, and adult grandchildren who had stories to tell and also laments for the lack of meaningful connections with other generations.

As well, I felt compelled to write this book because in this same cultural era in which generations feel this lack of meaningful connections with other generations, we find ourselves becoming a *five-generation society* in which multigenerational households are rapidly increasing across the North American landscape. Today more than 51.4 million Americans of all ages—or about one in six—live in multigenerational households. There is also a rise in grandparents caring for grandchildren, with 7 million grandparents living with a grandchild and approximately 3 million children being cared for primarily by that grandparent (*Five Facts about the Modern American Family*, Pew Research Center).

According to the United States Census Bureau's latest report on *Aging in the United States*, "between 2012 and 2050, the United States will experience considerable growth in its older population. In 2050, the population aged 65 and over is projected to be 83.7 million, almost double its estimated population of 43.1 million in 2012. The aging of the population will have wide-ranging implications for the country" (Census.gov/2014).

Studies such as one recorded by Bengston, Putney, and Harris in 2013 present the potential outcome of this emerging *five-generation society* being grandparents who will have an increasing influence on religious transmission, support, and socialization with their grandchildren in the twenty-first century (Roberto, 2015).

Finally, although I realize that some of the grandparents reading this book may feel alone in the journey due to such life experiences as death, divorce, partners who do not catch the vision, churches that do not support grandparenting faith, children who parent grandchildren in ways that do not create space to become the grandparent you desire to be, still I hope that you will find some richness in this book. I write this from the recognized privilege of having a spouse that shares my vision and my passion, as well as from the goodwill of having children who parent our grandchildren more intentionally and faithfully than we could have imagined (and who teach us, a little too late, how we could have been better parents ourselves).

To the company of those who read this book: I commit to pray for you on your journey as you share your own stories and I commit to pray for your grandchildren, be they biological or *grandchildren-in-faith*. In fact, even as I am in the process of writing, I am already praying for all the grandparents, grandchildren, parents, pastors, and others for whom I wrote this book!

1

Re-membering Our Place in the Story

All human communities live out some story that provides a context for understanding the meaning of history and gives shape and direction to their lives. If we allow the Bible to become fragmented, it is in danger of being absorbed into whatever other story is shaping our culture, and it will thus cease to shape our lives as it should.
—Craig Bartholomew and Michael Goheen, *The Drama of Scripture*

First a story, there should always be a story

A very long time ago, not long after the time of the great flood, the animals and the people began to spread out and inhabit the world. They made their homes primarily beside the great waters and along the great rivers that flowed through the land.

First there were small villages that grew into towns and some grew into mighty cities. Such was the case of the ancient city of Ur, located at the mouth of the Euphrates River on the Persian Gulf. Now, most of the people living in the ancient city of Ur believed in and worshiped multiple gods. There were gods of the river and gods of the trees, there were household gods and gods of the weather. There was, though, at least one family at that time and place that believed that there was only one God . . . one omnipotent and omnipresent God who was the God of all places and all things, a God who always was and always would be.

A man named Abram was a member of that family and along with his wife, Sarai, and all their household, they worshiped this God that they understood to be the one true God. As Abram went about his daily tasks he would take moments to come close to this God and this omnipresent God would come close to Abram.

One day God spoke to Abram and called him to leave the city of Ur so that, with his wife and their household, God called Abram to trust and to follow. I wonder how hard it was for Abram to trust the one God enough to leave all that he had ever known and follow God out into the unknown? I wonder how hard it was for Sarai to trust? But they did trust, and they packed up and left their home in Ur and followed God's call. They traveled down the long River Euphrates to the smaller city of Haran and there they set up camp and remained for some time until Abram again came close to God and God again came close to Abram and called him, along with his wife and household, to leave the safety of the river and follow God out into the unknown of the desert.

The desert is a strange and mysterious place. The wind blows and the landscape is always changing. In the daytime the desert is very hot and at night it is very cold. Would God be in such a place? Could the family of Abram and Sarai trust that God was calling them out for a purpose? When they came to a place called Shechem in the land of Canaan, Abram stepped out into a quiet place and again he came close to God and God came close to Abram; Abram knew that God was in that strange and mysterious place and so Abram found several smooth stones and built an altar. The altar remained so that when others traveled that way and saw the altar, they could also be reminded that God was in that place. I wonder if that altar still stands today?

The family traveled on and came to a place called Beth-el. Again Abram came close to God and God came close to Abram, and again Abram knew that God was in that place and he built an altar. After traveling and trusting and coming close to God for many, many more years, the household of Abram arrived at a place called Hebron, near the great oaks of Mamre, and this time when Abram came close to God he was standing on the edge of a great valley and looking out at all the night sky. He saw thousands and thousands of stars across the range of the universe, and when God came close to Abram this time, God made a covenant with the family of Abram, a promise that God would make of Abram and Sarai a great family. They would have as many children as the stars in the night sky. As a sign of this covenant, God changed Abram's name to Abraham (the father of a multitude) and changed Sarai's name to Sarah (pure, happy, princess of a multitude). But how could this be? Both Abraham and Sarah were very, very old by this time. Sarah laughed at the thought, but nine months later, their son Isaac was born. When Isaac was grown, old Sarah died and was laid to rest in the caves beside the oaks of Mamre. Abraham was also very, very old but still had one task left for God's purpose. Abraham sent his servant back to Haran, back along the River Euphrates, to bring back a suitable wife for his son Isaac.

After many months of travel, Rebekah returned with the servant and Isaac ran to meet her. Now Abraham's tasks were done and he died and was buried beside Sarah. Isaac and Rebekah took their place of worshiping and trusting the one true God. They had children and they told their children the story of God's covenant with Abraham and they remembered their place in God's great family. And on and on through the centuries, children were born and they were told the story of God's covenant and they were invited to remember their place in God's great family. Finally, after hundreds and hundreds of years and many generations, the covenant continues—as many as the stars in the night sky—and parents tell their children and their children become parents and tell their children and they become grandparents and the grandparents tell their children and their grandchildren about the covenant and they remember their place of belonging in God's great family of faithful who worship the one true God. But I wonder . . . are there some parents and grandparents and some children who have forgotten or never known or never been told of their place of belonging in the great family of God? And so they have forgotten who they are.

(Paraphrase of Berryman, *The Great Family, Godly Play*®, vol. 2.)

So we will not be forgotten in the deserts of life

Why begin this book on grandparenting faith with this ancient story of God's covenant with Abraham? Perhaps it is because the retelling of the ancient story of the covenant really gets to the essential point. It seems to me that too many people of the covenant have forgotten who they are and have forgotten to tell their children.

This book is not intended as a guilt trip for grandparents, but rather as an invitation to tell the great story of belonging. Our children and their children and the children yet unborn need to hear our stories of faithfulness, and they also need to hear our stories of lament. Sometimes it is simply by our willingness to tell our stories of failure that the realization of the depth of belonging to God's great family is really understood. This book is also an invitation to build altars in the world—in the world of our children and grandchildren—to remind us all that God is indeed in this place and God has not forgotten us in the deserts of life.

In the Old Testament, Psalm 78 begins with a warning:

> Give ear, O my people, to my teaching; incline your ears to the words of my mouth! 2 I will open my mouth in a parable; I will utter dark sayings from of old, 3 things that we have heard and known, that our fathers have told us. 4 We will not hide them from their children, but tell to the coming generation the glorious deeds of the Lord, and his might, and the wonders that he has done. 5 He established a testimony in Jacob and appointed a law in Israel, which he commanded our fathers to teach to their children, 6 that the next generation might know them, the children yet unborn and arise and tell them to their children, 7 so that they should set their hope in God and not forget the works of God, but keep his commandments; 8 and that they should not be like their fathers, a stubborn and rebellious generation, a generation whose heart was not steadfast, whose spirit was not faithful to God. (NRSV)

In centuries past, in fact for most of recorded history, households have lived and worked together. A sense of belonging to the previous generations and telling our stories was part of the fabric. But from the late nineteenth century a combination of cultural shifts, such as the industrial revolution, began to separate households to the point that, in the last few decades in our North American context of the late twentieth century we began to quickly and drastically lose connection with previous generations and their stories. And it should be of concern to all of us that the shift was not only in the surrounding culture; it was also taking place in our churches. Especially in the evangelical church, an accommodation to the mid-twentieth century cultural shift took place just about as rapidly as in the culture in general.

Before we even begin the theme of this book on grandparenting faith, it will help to take a step back for a brief look at cultural influencers and their impact on the role of grandparenting and on the role of the church in North America.

Although the history goes back further, let's make it simple and begin with what was taking place in 1950s America.

- One influence on the culture in general was technological advances. Modern conveniences such as washers and dryers, television, and air-conditioning moved the family indoors where they were no longer in view of neighbors. No need to hang out clothes on the line to dry, no need to sit on the front porch on summer evenings to cool off, and, with all the exciting stories on TV, no felt need for the family to sit around and tell stories anymore.

- Add to that the influence of mobility. Automobiles, along with improvements and efficiency in bus, train, and airplane travel, were all quickly opening up the world to us. No longer did families walk to the closest store to shop or to the nearest church to worship. With this mobility came choice as we had never known it before. Choice is a good thing; but interestingly, more choices in where to shop, what items were available to purchase, and what programs were being offered at that church across town, quickly led to an increasing value of consumerism. Grandparents may have had customer loyalty to the little corner store where they had always shopped or the neighborhood church where they had always worshiped; but that was then. Now we ask who offers the best bargains, the most variety, the best children's or youth programs at church, or the best school curriculum, and we arrive at a point where we value having access to the next, the best, and the latest.

- This improved technology and increased mobility were exacerbated with more post-war discretionary income and the advent of professional marketing. After World War II there was a manufacturing and economic boom across North America. More money entitled us to more technological conveniences, and more income increased our mobility and the desire for travel adventures. And with discretionary income came the advent of a previously unrecognized people group called teenagers. It was not until the early 1940s that the term *teenager* was coined, and corporate America quickly caught on and began to market directly to this demographic. This marketing to teens has continually and exponentially increased over the ensuing decades.

It appears that few of us may be willing to trade our conveniences, our travel, or our discretionary income for the sake of family relationships. I, along with most of you, still believe we can have it all. We want to travel! We love to travel! We wonder at times if we could survive without the convenience of our own car, let alone our own computer, our iPhone, iPad, and Kindle, or whatever other new technology has been invented by the time this book reaches publication. We like driving out of our way just to shop at Trader Joe's and then drop by Costco and maybe a quick stop at Target so we can have the choices that cater to our desires. But along with all this we also desire to keep our grandchildren close and tell them our family stories and tell them about God's covenant and their place in God's great family. But then, perhaps, we might also want to consider if all these community-disintegrating advancements in our culture might actually assist us in staying closer in our children and grandchildren's lives. That is a possibility; however, it is a possibility that demands we grandparents become more intentional.

The Intentionality of our story

There are always whispers of divinity in family conversations, but we need to listen carefully to be able to hear them. —Jerome Berryman, *Stories of God at Home*

Back in our grandparents' and great grandparents' days, sharing our lives and our stories just happened—or at least we assumed it just happened. We really didn't give it much, if any, intentional thought. Grandkids lived next door or down the street in cities or small towns or with us on the farm. Life happened and kids knew the story or at least the basic DNA of the family to which they belonged. For the most part, families of all generations did chores together, grandmas taught kids to bake pies and sew quilts and tend gardens—rarely intentionally but rather out of necessity. Today if we grandparents are not intentionally seeking ways to tell our family story, do life together, mentor our grandkids to tend gardens and make homemade pies, and create places of belonging, it most likely won't happen—at least it won't happen as easily. The challenge comes in making technology, mobility, discretionary income, and the proliferation of choice work *for* us instead of working against us in sharing our lives and our stories and our faith stories with our busy grandchildren.

RE-MEMBERING OUR PLACE IN THE STORY

Re-membering dis-membered generations

At our birth we are named, not numbered. The name is that part of speech by which we are recognized as a person: We are not classified as a species of animal. We are not labeled as a compound of chemicals. We are not assessed for our economic potential and given a cash value. We are named. What we are named is not as significant as that we are named. —Eugene Peterson, *Run with the Horses*

In a public lecture given at Regent College (Vancouver, BC) in 2002 on *The Way of Wisdom from the Book of Proverbs*, Dr. Bruce Waltke made the statement that "we have effectively dis-membered our children by stripping them of the memories they so desperately need." These terms—*dis-membering* and *re-membering*—paint vivid word pictures of what we do to ourselves and our families when we are not intentional about reminding ourselves that we are members of something so much bigger and ultimately more important than our daily activities of life. Every time we tell the stories of our family and the stories of the people who have trusted God—our functional great-grandparents of faith down through church history—we are in effect re-membering ourselves and our children to our true identity, purpose, and direction for life, and potentially re-membering ourselves to our place of belonging in God's great, covenant family.

In her book, *Family Ministry: A Comprehensive Guide*, Diana Garland writes about this intentional need for making family connections and memories. "A house," she writes, "is furnished with furniture: a home is furnished with memories." Just this one thought on being intentional may mean that we make a conscious decision not to create a designer home to show off to friends, but rather create a home that bears witness to our identity and our family identity. Our consumer-saturated culture (think of those great tchotchke finds at HomeGoods or Crate and Barrel) creates desires to stage our homes for compliments instead of creating spaces for memory making. Sad to admit, but coordinating colors and styles dictated by the latest designers may not really be what our grandkids need from us.

What is the reality of generational and relational dis-membering in church and in families in the twenty-first century and what might it look like—even visually—to create an alternative worldview in which to live and relate as generations together?

This question reminds me to stop and take a closer look not only at my own life choices, but also at the church's accommodation of the surrounding cultural shifts over the past sixty or so years. What impacts have the shifts in technology, mobility, discretionary income, marketing, consumerism, and proliferation of choice had on the North American church's ability to draw generations together as Christ's family? More than ever the wisdom to be intentional in our own actions with our own grandchildren as well as our grandchildren-in-faith that are growing up in our churches. The church is supremely situated to be a prime support system for the roles of grandparents in our children's rapidly changing world.

In what ways might the church in North American have effectively dis-membered a generation or so of young people among whom are some of our children and grandchildren? In his book *When the Church Was a Family: Recapturing Jesus' Vision for Authentic Christian Community*, Joseph Hellerman points out that the Bible creates a worldview of people as the family of God, an authentic community where faith is lived out in the intergenerational family, clan, and tribe, as it is referred to in Scripture. For most of the history of humanity, children have been typically raised by tribes, clans, and variously extended networks of kin (Kornhaber and Woodward, 1985). For most of ancient as well as modern history the local church has taken that role; however, with the shifting of cultural values of mobility, proliferation of choice, consumerism, individualism, added to human developmental research and schooling models, the church has come to be seen in the way that Tod Bolsinger puts it in his book *It Takes a Church to Raise A Christian: How the Community of God Transforms Lives*: "culturally, we have come to think of the church as a dispenser of resources to help the individual on his or her Christian journey—come here and choose from our wide array of Christian classes, teachings, and activities that you need to live out your individual Christian life. The church is God's incarnation today. The Church is Jesus' body on earth." In chapter one of my book *Kingdom Family: Re-Envisioning God's Plan for Marriage and Family*, I write more about the value of re-envisioning the church's role as God's great family to which we are called to belong. Many Americans have been trained to become consumers of church and trained to see the church as a cultural service provider rather than a community of the faithful living a biblical model of the kingdom of God (Okholm, 2012).

Though in the rest of this book I will make recommendations, share practical ideas for intentional grandparenting, and relate stories of successes and failures, we need to start here: our grandchildren as well as our grandchildren-in-faith need role models of a better way of being re-membered to a larger faith community. Tod Bolsinger is correct, it does take a church to raise a Christian (Bolsinger, 2004) and all the great stories and advice we can give on doing it individually is somewhat undermined if the church does not recognize the importance of intergenerational community and the value of grandparenting faith.

Ross Parsley, founder and lead pastor of ONEchapel in Austin, Texas and the author of *Messy Church: A Multigenerational Mission for God's Family*, suggests that God sees the church less like a social organization that does good things for the community or like a spiritual and self-help counseling center and more like a family—a multigenerational group of real people who love each other and care for one another's needs and one another's children and grandchildren—no matter how messy. "We are not consumers asking what the church can do for us. We are family members learning how to love deeply, fight fairly, and share selflessly with others. Imagine the generations working together, combining the experience, wisdom, and resources of age with the strength, enthusiasm, and innovation of youth. It's messy, but full of hope and healing for a generation starving to belong to something greater than themselves" (Parsley, 2012, back cover).

So I invite you to read ahead, hopeful that you will recognize, support, and encourage the church and your community to come alongside grandparents of all stripes as we re-member ourselves together in our role and our responsibility to love our kids—no matter their age—telling them the messy stories of our lives and telling them anew the old, old story of God's covenant and inviting them in to find their place of belonging in God's great family.

Bridge 1: Stories of Connection

Personal stories from ordinary grandparents on remembering our place in God's story.

Faith Tradition . . . *by Mary Kauffman*

One of my sons and his family live in another state, and periodically I take short trips to visit them. On one particular trip a few years ago, my son accompanied me to Mass, even though he was not practicing his Catholic faith at that time. An announcement was made of a music program to be held in the church that evening, and children especially were invited; I suggested we attend and bring his eldest child, five-year-old Maddie, to hear the concert. He agreed.

Maddie had never been in a Catholic church before. When we first walked in the door, she stopped mid-walk, eyes opened wide, to take in all the color, all the stained glass, the flowers around the altar, the statues surrounding the sanctuary. She then noticed the Stations of the Cross on the wall and rather than being repulsed or frightened, as some might expect, she was enthralled.

Taking her father's hand, she began tugging him to follow her around the side aisles of the church so he could tell her the whole story—What is happening to this man? Why are people hurting him? Who is he? Who are the other people? What is he carrying? What is on his head? She looked and listened, scene by scene, fascinated, transfixed, engrossed by the story. We then sat down to listen to the concert. (When we went back to their home, her mother asked her about the evening, and she said she had learned about Cheese's mother.)

About a year later, our son returned to the faith he had been raised in, full of renewed enthusiasm and spirit. Who knows what seeds were planted by a child's vision and interest in something that touched her spirit on her first visit to a church? My son's indulgence in granting my request to return to the evening music program and a child's fascination with the visuals of faith became a trinitarian generational experience that rekindled a continuance of our family's faith tradition, one of the strongest bonds in our familial history.

Passing on a Blessing . . . *by Susan Ballard*

What a joy it was and still is to be a grandmother! I have many happy memories from my grandparents and decided that I wanted to pass a blessing of happy memories on to my grandkids, so I have created their lives in picture books.

Back in 1996, when my first grandchild was born, I started taking photos and making albums for her. As more grandchildren were added, I continued to take photos and create albums of their lives, starting with pictures of their moms at their baby showers before they were even born!

I now have six grandkids. My first has ten small 4 x 6 albums with 100 pictures in each. In our current digital world, when so many pictures never make it off a cell phone, it is important not to leave pictures in my phone or camera but to get them printed and dates on the back as soon as possible; otherwise the task gets too overwhelming. Because I have made this a priority over the years, my grandkids look forward to pulling out their albums when they come to visit and get to remember the fun times of their past years and we get to share the stories of those times together.

I am still filling albums for all six grandchildren. I try to take group pictures when I can and also put in as many pictures from both their parent's side of the family when possible. This was and still is not a chore for me, but remains a fun, ongoing project!

I also love to journal, so my grandkids can someday read the happenings and history of their lives through the eyes of their grandmother.

I lost my husband to Parkinson's in 2011 and now I am so happy that our grandkids will be able to see pictures of their past with their grandfather as well as past grandparents and great-grandparents that were part of their lives and their stories.

I hope the albums will be a blessing in their lives as they grow up, bringing back memories, sharing stories, and remembering the family to which they belong.

Prayers for re-membering dis-membered families and broken relationships

---

A prayer of praise for belonging~

Gracious Lord, my hope and my history!
What a beautiful thing it is to belong to a story so ancient and
 so wild and wonderful, so hard and also so hopeful!
Thank you for the expectation and privilege you have given to me
 to tell that story with my grandchildren.

BRIDGE 1: STORIES OF CONNECTION

I pray for deep roots and hearts filled with hope and home for all
> the children in my life.

It is indeed a wonderous thing to belong!

There are too many people in this world who don't know
> the story of their belonging and so they despair.

Lord, may I become a storyteller of hope and tradition
> and thus give my grandchildren a foundation of faithfulness.
> Amen

A prayer for sharing our stories~

Dear Heavenly Father of us all.
In your holy word you have commanded us
> to tell our stories to each new generation.

You established a testimony in Jacob and appointed
> a law in Israel,

which commanded our fathers to teach to their children
> so that the next generation might know them, that
> the children yet unborn too might arise

and tell them to their children
> so they might set their hope in God
> and not forget the works of God,

but keep your commandments.

We pray that our children, our grandchildren
> and those that come after them

should not be like others,
> a stubborn and rebellious generation,
> a generation whose heart was not steadfast,

whose spirit was not faithful to God.

May we remember our place in the story
> so that we might

re-member our grandchildren
> to places of belonging and places of hope. Amen

THE GRAND-PARENTING EFFECT

A prayer for those who have become dis-membered in our lives~

Dear Lord, I fear that I may be too late . . . but more than that,
I fear that I will take upon myself all the responsibility,
    all the guilt.
Lord, help me to breathe . . . help me to be still and know
    that you are God and I am not.

I alone cannot force, coerce, or guilt my children nor my
    grandchildren.
Give me grace to remember that my place is only to love
    and to know
that that love shows up best when it is unconditional.
So let me fall on that grace you so freely bestow
and learn to live and love in the tension of that grace. Amen

---

What were you thinking, Lord?

(A mother's prayer from Melody Carlson,
Lost Boys and the Moms Who Love Them)

Lord, some days your gift of children makes me despair.
I sometimes feel these children are walking proof that
I failed at my most important job of life.
You created life through me and so I expected the joyful rewards
    of parenthood, of a family. And now this.

Why did you make parenting so difficult?
Why did you make a mother's heart so ready to give all,
    hope all, believe all . . . and yet so ready to break?
Why couldn't you make love safe?

Lord, I need to be a source of nurture and encouragement,
    of wisdom and grace, but I'm feeling weak and afraid.
And I don't want to break anymore.

BRIDGE 1: STORIES OF CONNECTION

Help me. Be strength for me. Be a refuge for my family.
Be a net of safety under us. And if my heart should break again,
    make all the pieces beautiful for your purposes.
(Especially now . . . for my grandchildren.) Amen.

A prayer for prodigals~

Dear Lord, How I wish I could still protect my children
    and grandchildren from accident and harm,
from disease—physical and emotional disease—
    and also from spiritual disease.
I wish I could save them from the influences
    of the wrong crowd and bad decisions;
from all the daily threats
    to body, mind, soul, and spirit that are part of our world.

But. I. Can't.

So, dear Lord, I kneel before you today in great need.
Only you can see my children and grandchildren every moment.
Are you watching over them? Do they care?
Even when you walk with them through the valley of death
    will they have eyes to see?
Ears to hear your spirit whisper to them,
Not that way—this way. Walk here?

Please send your angels as ministering spirits to guard them.
And as for me, let me bask in the peace that comes from trusting
    your mighty hand to save. Amen.

A prayer for a world that is changing~

Gracious God.
The world is moving too fast and changing too quickly.
It is hard for us all to remember who we are
    and where we came from
    and too hard to imagine where we're going.

THE GRAND-PARENTING EFFECT

I confess, Lord, that sometimes I feel like yelling,
Stop the train! I want to get off!

But wouldn't it be great if I could be the calm the world needs?
And create the spaces of reliability my grandkids need?
What if, gracious God, I could offer a refuge in the midst
    of the chaos?

Lord, St. Francis-like I pray, make me an instrument
    of your peace.
Where there is hatred, let me sow love—
where there is injury, pardon—
where doubt, faith—
where despair, hope—
darkness, light—sadness, joy.
In my role as grandparent—and an aging grandparent at that
    —grant that
I may not so much seek to be consoled by my children
    and grandchildren as to console,
    or to be understood as to understand.
Because, as I mentioned before, dear Lord . . .
    wouldn't it be great
if I could be the calm the world, and especially
    my grandkids, need?

2

Building Bridges, Planting Seeds

An old man going a lone highway,
Came, at the evening cold and gray, to a chasm vast and deep and wide.
Through which was flowing a sullen tide.
The old man crossed in the twilight dim, the sullen stream had no fear for him;
But he turned when safe on the other side and built a bridge to span the tide.
Old man, said a fellow pilgrim near, You are wasting your strength with building here;
Your journey will end with the ending day, you never again will pass this way;
you've crossed the chasm, deep and wide, why build this bridge at evening tide?
The builder lifted his old gray head, Good friend, in the path I have come, he said,
There followed after me to-day a youth whose feet must pass this way.
This chasm that has been as naught to me to that fair-haired youth may a pitfall be;
He, too, must cross in the twilight dim; good friend,
I am building this bridge for him! —Will Allen Dromgoole

Your stories may look like seeds that have landed lifelessly among the cracks in the pavement,
but they are putting down their roots, silently breaking through the hardness,
and will bear fruit and new life. —Sam Greenlee (Facebook post)

THE GRAND-PARENTING EFFECT

Bridging islands and planting seeds: why both are important

As I often do when grandkids visit, I pulled my *parable box* out of the garage. It is just a large Paris rectangular flap box from Michael's Crafts Store that I have spray-painted gold. I use it for telling my grandchildren—and other children—parables from the Bible. Why? Because parables are gifts that God gives us that are precious like gold; however, parables also have lids (like this gold parable box) that need to come off before we truly receive them as gifts. So, we have to open them up and play with them a bit before they really belong to us.

This time, as I always do when telling parables, I open the lid carefully and look quickly inside and say . . .

Yep, just as we thought. This is a parable. Parables are precious like gold—and this box is gold. Parables are mysterious like gifts—and just like all gifts, we need to open them up and look inside, take out what is inside and explore what this parable gift might really be.

Parables are like gifts that God gives us. Sometimes it is hard to figure out the gift inside the box, sometimes we have to put our thinking caps on and think really hard and we still might not understand what this gift might really be.

So we try again—perhaps at a later time—to open this gift. We take the lid off, explore the parable inside, and even though we don't completely understand this parable, we know that it really is a gift and that it really does already belong to us, and each time we open this gift from God we understand it a little bit more deeply than we did the first few times.

Once as Jesus was teaching beside the Sea of Galilee, he told three parables about seeds so the people might begin to understand what the kingdom of God is really like. Jesus told a parable of the sower and the seeds, he told the parable of the mustard seed, and he also told this parable about a farmer and the growing seed.

From the gold parable box I take a row of seeds (a simple string of tiny beads sewn to a golden brown felt strip). Next I take out the farmer with his bag of seed, then I sit back and feel the story forming in my soul . . .

Jesus said: *The kingdom of God is like someone who scatters seed on the ground . . . and then goes home . . . and sleeps . . . and gets up.*

The farmer comes day after day to see if the seeds sprout and grow. Morning and evening, day after day he comes. The farmer does not know how it happens—how the earth produces of itself, first the sprout . . . (Now I roll out light green felt with tiny green felt sprouts attached but we can still see the row of seeds below.) We sit back—my grandchildren and I—and wonder at how tiny seeds grow into soft, green sprouts. *I bet the farmer wonders also.* (I roll out another felt, this time a darker green with stalks just above the soft and lighter green sprouts and both just above the tiny seeds all in a row.) . . . And I say, *then the stalks appear . . . and then the head and then the full grain in the head.* (I roll out a golden felt strip and trace the golden threads of the full grain in the heads. This time I take the farmer in my hands and place the sickle at his side.) . . . And I say, *when the grain is ripe, at once the farmer gathers it with his sickle because the harvest has come.*

And again, we stop and wonder . . .

> *We wonder what the farmer is doing when he is not sleeping and getting up while the grain is growing.*
>
> *We wonder how the farmer feels trusting the seed to the earth and to the sun and the rain.*
>
> *We wonder if the farmer pays any attention to the grain while it is growing.*
>
> *We wonder how the farmer feels about the grain when it is ready to harvest.*
>
> *We wonder what this parable really means.*
>
> *We wonder what the kingdom of God might really be.*
>
> *We wonder how this little parable helps us to imagine what the kingdom of God might really be.*

(Paraphrased from Stewart, 2000, 82–85.)

I wonder how often you've planted seeds for your grandchildren to discover and waited patiently for those tiny seeds to bear fruit? A lot of grandparenting is just planting seeds and releasing control. Sometimes that other *seed parable* may feel more appropriate to your life situation. You know the one, where the farmer goes out and scatters seeds that sometimes fall on hard ground, or packed soil, or among the weeds. As grandparents, we usually don't have the control that parents have, or at least think they have. What sort of seeds do you plant? Kingdom seeds? Seeds of hope? Assurance? Challenge? Perhaps seeds of belonging to something and someone bigger than right here and right now? Seeds of parables that Jesus told so long ago . . . and keeps telling today for those who have ears to listen? My friend, Phyllis—whose story is in the bridge following chapter four—discovered that just by virtue of her place of connection—a safe place of connection—she is invited into her granddaughter's wondering about the mysteries of life. Phyllis has proven herself a safe person, and now she can get away with planting and nourishing seeds in her grandchildren's lives that the parents might never be invited to plant or nourish.

This planting and nourishing seeds does not simply take place with our biological grandchildren, but also with young people in the neighborhood, in church, in mentoring relationships formal or not so formal. I have found this true in my own experience. Being an older—and hopefully wiser—person in someone's life is an invitation for seed planting. Mostly it is not all that hard to toss out the seeds and pay attention to where they land and then nourish them with a little wondering. You just need to pay attention and have a few seeds ready to toss out at a moment's notice, right?

Both analogies—seeds and bridges—create space for influence. Both have the power to connect the dots between our lives and our grandchildren's lives. Both bridge building and seed planting have the potential of changing the internal culture that forms our grandchildrens' worldview.

Worldviews are formed by the culture in which we live, our *cultural ethos*. Culture is an interesting thing and holds so much power of influence in the way we see and understand our world and ourselves. There are really two planes of culture in our lives. There is the external culture—the surrounding culture formed by politics and media. We often refer to this as *pop culture* and often blame it for all life's ills. Then there's another plane of influence, another culture that has power to form our way of seeing the world, this is usually referred to as *internal* culture or *family* culture.

Creating internal culture or wringing our hands over the impact of pop culture

In chapter one of this book I listed a few of the major cultural values that vie for the attention of our hearts and minds as well as the hearts and minds of our grandchildren. One of the ways that Merriam-Webster defines culture is "the customary beliefs, social forms, and material traits of a racial, religious, or social group." Some of us are guilty of defining culture as some force of change or demand for conformity from which we need to protect our children/grandchildren. When we become more concerned with protecting our grandchildren *from* the culture, we just might miss opportunities for bridging the gaps or nourishing the seeds we've planted. The bottom line is that the more intentionally we offer our children an embodiment of our customary beliefs, social forms, and material traits from our family stories, our faith stories, and our belonging with consistency to a certain social group, the stronger their identity and embodiment of that *internal culture* becomes, and the surrounding *pop culture* will define them less. Perhaps the mind-set of engaging our grandchildren with the stories, beliefs, traditions, and rituals of their family's *internal culture* is more influential and effective than the mind-set of somehow bubble-wrapping our grandchildren from the *external culture* in which they are living and growing up? In other words, the more they begin to view the world around them through the lens of their own *internal culture*, the more they, in turn, will have the power to transform the world.

Sometimes as grandparents we have the potential to create an alternative *lens* through which our grandchildren—and we ourselves—see the world around us. Unfortunately, the reality is that sometimes grandparents are denied that potential to build bridges between *external culture* and *internal culture*. I will address that later in this chapter; however, much of the time it is simply a case of grandparents not considering the potential power they have to influence their grandchildren's worldview.

The practice of seeing our world through bifocals

Diana Garland, former dean of the Baylor School of Social Work at Baylor University, defines the term *culture* as referring to the core values an identifiable people group shares with one another. These core values explain the way we behave with one another. Culture touches all aspects of our lives—what we consider beautiful, what we consider right and wrong, how we are entertained, even what decisions we make. The issues of culture bring us face to face with the reality that we can never step outside of our own culturally tinted lenses to *see* another culture objectively (Garland, 2012, 285).

How do we step outside and recognize our own biases? Do you ever wonder what those cultural biases keep us from seeing? Perhaps the important question to ask here is how to begin to construct bridges that encourage our grandchildren to step beyond the cultural biases that keep them from really *seeing* and cross the bridge connecting them to an alternative story, a story that can bridge the gap between all that came before them and all who will come after.

How do we begin to construct bridges from which they might see the world around them through an alternative *lens*? Or better yet, how do we create an invitation for the practice of seeing their lives through *bifocals*. It is important to remember, however, that the goal is not to remove ourselves or our children from the culture; rather it is to gift them with observation.

Today, as in most of history, family practices and traditions serve as a means of creating what Garland calls *family culture* or internal culture— an *internal culture that exists within an external culture* and that transmits values and creates meaning. The bottom line here is to realize that the stronger and more defined our internal family culture, the less power the external culture has in shaping our worldview. In the bridge following this chapter, I give you a list of intentional ideas for strengthening your internal family culture.

The reality is that families with more defined ethnic heritage are usually better at this than the rest of us—better at transmitting practices and traditions that create meaning for their children and grandchildren. Obviously, I don't know where you are coming from; however, I come from a long line of middle-class white folks who need to work a little harder at transmitting what it means to be us. But lest my children and grandchildren lose sight of the values and traditions that make us Okholms, we have to be more intentional about creating *internal culture* in our family.

Like neighboring islands without any bridges

In the introduction of this book I told the story about Jerome Berryman, who worked as part of an interdisciplinary team caring for suicidal children and their families. The team was made up of a psychiatrist, a psychologist, a social worker, an MD drug expert, and Berryman, an Episcopal priest. Together their team provided family systems therapy and studied what had gone wrong in family relationships that resulted in children trying to commit suicide. As they interviewed more and more family units, they began to discover the common thread was in the lack of stories told to one another. They did not tell stories about vacations, funny things that happened, sad things, grandparents, births, deaths, pets, hopes, trips, dreams, heritage, or any other tales that planted seeds of *internal family culture*. Their communication was reduced to commands, demands, exclamations, brief explanations, and questions requiring short, factual answers. "The family members," wrote Berryman, "were like neighboring islands without any bridges. There were no narratives bridging the gaps and connecting them, no pathways to create a sense of belonging and meaning for individuals in that setting" (Berryman, 2018, 22).

Our stories become our habits, our habits become our traditions, and our traditions ground us in something bigger than the latest cultural fad. We and our children/grandchildren are more equipped to step outside and observe the surrounding *pop culture* as we are told stories, practice our family habits, experience our family traditions, and practice *seeing* the world through the *lens* of our *family's internal culture*. Later in this book I write a lot more about habits, traditions, and rituals that arise from the practice of seeing the world through a Christian lens; however, for the purpose of this chapter I now turn our attention to finding the balance between exposing our grandchildren to the world or overprotecting our grandchildren from the world. Trying to find balance between the two takes up a lot of our mental imagination these days. How much we do we expose them, and more importantly, what are we exposing them to? How much protecting is *overprotecting* and what are we protecting them from? Taking time to *name* what it is we are exposing to or protecting from plays a large part in how we build bridges between the islands we may become.

Overprotective or intentional?
It can become a fine line to navigate

It is possible to drown children and adults in a constant flow of stimuli, forcing them to spend so much energy responding to the outside world that the inward life and the creative imagination which flows from it become stunted or atrophied. —Elise Boulding

---

Posted as an Instagram story by the mother of our granddaughters:

[Sometimes] people get really worked up about how sheltered my kids are and how overprotective I must be because they haven't seen the Disney oeuvre by age seven and because we don't let them watch whatever show, but those [same] people don't seem to give the same weight to:

- *Teaching my children about white privilege and how to be respectfully race conscious*

- *Teaching them that they are allowed to take up space and speak up*
- *Teaching them that no means no*
- *Taking them to museums to learn about other cultures and other times*
- *Teaching them nature awareness and creation care*
- *Introducing them to the great artists and composers*
- *Making sure they spend time around different kinds of people*
- *Having conversations about why there's often only one female character in a show or why the prince was so rude and she still fell in love with him or why is bad equated with fat or ugly or old in cartoons or what advertisers do to us to make us want their product.*

Michael Chabon, Pulitzer Prize-winning author of various books and novels including *The Final Solution, Wonder Boys,* and *Summerland,* wrote about childhood's lost wilderness. He asks the question, "What price in imagination will today's children pay for our over-protectiveness?" (*The Week,* 2009).

Although it might seem contradictory for me to quote my daughter's lament above and then turn around and start writing about Chabon's article on "Childhood's Lost Wilderness" and the price today's children pay for our overprotectiveness, I believe that my daughter and Chabon are communicating the same challenge. Let me explain.

Chabon writes about growing up in a home that backed up to a woods—woods that in his imagination were filled with unfathomable shadows and potentially scary things. Along with learning the history of his hometown in school, that history of what happened in the past brought inspiration and made those woods a magical space. "You could work [history] into your games, your imaginings, your lonely flights from the turmoil or torpor of your life at home. My friends and I spent hours there being braves, crusaders, commandos, blues and grays."

He goes on to say that "most great stories of adventure, from *The Hobbit* to *Seven Pillars of Wisdom,* come furnished with a map." His map contained all the places he and his friends could explore in 1970s Maryland. "Every story of adventure is in part the story of a landscape, of the interrelationship between human beings (or hobbits, as the case may be) and topography. Every adventure story is conceivable only with reference to the particular set of geographical features that in each case sets the course, literally, of the tale. People read stories of adventure—and write them—because they have themselves been adventurers. Childhood is, or has been, or ought to be, the great original adventure, a tale of privation, courage, constant vigilance, danger, and sometimes calamity."

The woods and creek beds, the alleys and hiking trails of our world have been abandoned in favor of a system of *reservations* at entertainment destinations—think Disney World, Discovery Zone, Chuck E. Cheese—or as Chabon names them, "jolly internment centers mapped and planned by adults with no blank spots aside from doors marked *staff only*." Unplanned and unguarded exploration, little imagination and the risk of figuring it out yourself is required. Chabon goes on to explain the rationale behind this curtailing of adventure, this "closing off of *Wilderness*" and increased anxiety we all feel over the abduction of children by strangers, this "fear of wolves in the wilderness." He gives statistics: for example, a 1999 study by the Justice Department that reported the number of abductions by strangers in the United States was 115; ironically, that is about the same rate per year that such crimes have historically occurred. In other words, being a child is exactly no more and no less dangerous than it ever was. (This statistic does not include the increase of school shootings. That subject will not be directly addressed in this chapter.) What has changed is the fanatic media reporting. "At times it seems as if parents [and grandparents] are being deliberately encouraged to fear for their children's [and grandchildren's] lives, though only a cynic would suggest there was money to be made in doing so."

> The endangerment of children—that persistent theme of our lives, arts, and literature over the past 20 years—resonates so strongly because, as parents, as members of preceding generations, we look at the poisoned legacy of modern industrial society and its ills, at the world of strife and radioactivity, climatological disasters, overpopulation, and commodification, and feel guilty—our children have become cult objects to us, too precious to be risked. At the same time they have become fetishes, the objects of unhealthy and diseased fixation. And once something is fetishized, capitalism steps in and finds a way to sell it. (Chabon, 2009, 65)

I wonder how easily we contain our children and grandchildren within the confines of amusement parks and entertainment venues, video games and the Disney Channel in the name of safe entertainment and venues, assuming we are both protecting them and at the same time exposing them to a wider world? And in consideration of how Chabon's article and my daughter's lament are complementary, I wonder if by *overprotecting* our kids we are actually keeping them from the adventures and stories they so desperately need to grow up well. I wonder if we are inadvertently exposing them to capitalism with a myriad of passive entertainment designed to sell them products and lifestyle. I will talk more about consumerism in the next chapter; however, for the rest of this chapter I hope to give you pause to reflect on some new proactive research on children and the benefits a grandparent might offer by way of exposing grandchildren to some of the topics my daughter listed above.

The inverse power of praise or why heaping praise on our grandchildren may not work

Do not ask your children to strive for extraordinary lives.
Such striving may seem admirable, but it is the way of foolishness.
Help them instead to find the wonder and the marvel of an ordinary life.
Show them the joy of tasting tomatoes, apples and pears.
Show them how to cry when pets and people die.
Show them the infinite pleasure in the touch of a hand.
And make the ordinary come alive for them.
The extraordinary will take care of itself. —William Martin

Remember those popular bumper stickers that started appearing on many of the SUVs in neighborhoods around the 1980s, such as "my child is an honor student" or "proud parent of a star student"? This, along with handing out awards just for being you and all the other hype of the self-esteem movement were taking our nation by storm in the 1980s and 1990s when some of us were raising children. That late twentieth-century *self-esteem storm* has left in its wake too many unmotivated, self-centered, entitled, anxious, and depressed youth and young adults. Basically, what was taking place during those decades was a presumption that if we simply gave our children—and grandchildren—enough praise, they would succeed in life. The irony of this thinking is what science journalists Po Bronson and Ashley Merryman label *the inverse power of praise*.

About a decade ago Bronson and Merryman researched why many of modern society's strategies for nurturing children are in fact backfiring because key twists in the science of child development had been—and in many instances still are being—overlooked. Their research is documented and published in their 2009 book, *NurtureShock: New Thinking About Children*, in which they reflect on the inverse power of praise, why insufficient sleep adversely affects kids' capacity to learning, why white parents don't talk about race, why kids lie, why evaluation methods for giftedness and accompanying programs don't work, and why siblings really fight. I will not touch on all these topics, referring you instead to their book; however, I do think that as grandparents who desire to create intentional bridges between the generations, we will want to consider those themes that have worked in our surrounding culture to create disconnection between generations and turn us into islands that share the same family without sharing our lives and stories.

According to Bronson and Merryman's research, there are at least two downsides of praising our children or grandchildren too much. One downside is that having high self-esteem actually *does not* improve grades or career achievement. And in some cases, adults who were praised too often as they grew up were more prone to increased alcohol usage, aggression, and depression (Dweck,1999; Bronson and Merryman, 2009, 15–25).

A leading proponent of the self-esteem movement in the last part of the twentieth century, Dr. Roy Baumeister, concluded after much research that the self-esteem movement was not only flawed, it was in many cases detrimental to the health and mental well-being of those who had grown up during that era. In 2005 he helped publish research showing that for college students on the verge of failing in class, esteem-building praise causes their grades to sink further. Baumeister was quoted as saying that these findings were "the biggest disappointment of my career" (Baumeister et al., 2005; Bronson and Merryman, 2009, 18).

Grandparents are known for heaping praise on grandchildren; that's just recognized as part of the perks of grandparenting. But a couple of things happen when we constantly praise. First, we help create *praise junkies*. A praise junkie is a person who grows up getting too frequent rewards and therefore not acquiring persistence. They have been programmed by so much praise with little effort that they quit trying when the rewards disappear. We set our children's brain up for actual chemical need for constant reward (Cloninger, 2004). An opposite effect of praise is the finding by Dr. Carol Dweck (1999) that frequently praised children are often more competitive and more interested in tearing others down. Image maintenance becomes their primary concern (Bronson and Merryman, 2009, 21–26).

Still another impact of too much praise relates to the well-known research on moral development by Lawrence Kohlberg (1958, et al.) who studied the stages humans go through in developing moral reasoning. The natural progression moves from *egocentrism*—it is all about me (the self being the center of one's universe) to *sociocentrism*—the recognition of law and order, reward and punishment, and need for fairness in relationship to others. The highest stage of moral reasoning is considered by Kohlberg to be a form of *theocentrism*—the realization that how I relate to self and others has more to do with a higher authority and the need to live by principles rather than by what serves me best or because I fear getting caught. The more adults praise and reward without merit, the less likely our children/grandchildren will move to higher stages of moral reasoning and remain stunted between *egocentrism* and *sociocentrism*. The ability for moral reasoning may be directly linked to how much we allow our children to be challenged in both their education and their life experiences.

Cultivating compassion just might be one of the greatest gifts a grandparent can bestow . . .

Love and compassion are necessities, not luxuries. Without them, humanity cannot survive. —Dalai Lama XIV, *The Art of Happiness*

What separates privilege from entitlement is gratitude. —Brené Brown

---

It is time we take a brief look at the concept of *entitlement*. The dictionary defines it as "the belief that one is inherently deserving of privilege or special treatment." Entitlement looks like impatience, pouting or sulking, laziness, not sharing, tantrums, blaming, or glaring when one does not get their way. Entitlement sounds like, *I deserve . . .* or *if she has it, I need to have it also!* Entitlement is an example of living within an *egocentric* stage of morality per Kohlberg. It is normal for all children to go through this developmental stage; however, the danger comes when any of us gets stuck there. As long as our children/grandchildren can demand, throw tantrums, and sulk their way into getting what they think they must have lest they die, they will remain stuck in that lowest stage of moral development. The ironic thing about entitlement is that even children that appear to have successfully moved from *egocentric* to *sociocentric* stage of moral development will often devolve back to a lower level in their teen or even adult years when not presented with models, challenges, and opportunities to express gratitude and compassion.

We have a lot of adults walking around today that have cycled downward rather than upward and so continue to function at what might be referred to as a second-stage *egocentrism*. Some of them might even be your children or grandchildren. Robert Cloninger, a professor at Washington University in St. Louis, trained rats and mice in mazes to have persistence by carefully *not* rewarding them when they got to the finish. "The key is intermittent reinforcement," says Cloninger. The brain has to learn that frustrating spells can be worked through. "A person who grows up getting too frequent rewards will not have persistence, because they will quit when the rewards disappear. Jumping in with praise is like jumping in too soon with the answer to a homework problem, as it robs our children from the chance to make the deduction for themselves." But what if the child makes the wrong conclusion: Can I really leave this up to him, at his age? Po Bronson gives the example of this with raising his own son. He writes, "I'm still an anxious parent. This morning, I tested [his son] on the drive to school by asking: What happens to your brain, again, when it gets to think about something hard? [His son's response:] 'It gets bigger, like a muscle'" (Cloninger, 2004; Bronson and Merryman, 2009, 24).

How do we create environments for our grandchildren to begin thinking outside of themselves and caring for others? For a start, try resisting the urge to tell them how amazing they are all the time. Occasionally is perfect, especially when tempered by opportunities to struggle. When tempted to go for comments like, *You did a great job in your little league game today! You are amazing!* or *You are an artist! That is a beautiful picture you drew!*, try substituting phrases such as, *I bet you had fun at the game today! I wonder if the other players did also? I wonder how the other team felt when they lost?* or, *Drawing is fun, I wonder if you might like to tell me about your picture?* Perhaps even going a step further by beginning to look for opportunities to create compassion in your grandchildren. I have listed some practical ideas for doing just that in the bridge following this chapter.

Brené Brown, whom I quote several times in this chapter, is famous for her speaking and writing about vulnerability, worthiness, shame, and other emotions running underneath daily life for most of us living under our current cultural ethos. One of the themes she returns to again and again is the importance of cultivating empathy. Cultivating empathy strengthens our capacity for compassion. It is important to realize that although we often think of empathy and sympathy together, as Brown is quick to explain, they are quite different qualities. For one thing, she says that empathy consists of four qualities: the ability to take the perspective of another person, staying away from judgment, recognizing emotion in others, and communicating it.

Brown defines empathy as *feeling with people* and points out that it is a *vulnerable choice* for us because it requires a person to tap into something personal that identifies with the struggle of another.

Our grandchildren have opportunities to learn empathy from their parents as well as from their teachers and peers; however, the practice of empathy can be especially influential when it is learned from the stories of a grandparent's life experiences. Grandparents have a particular advantage on this front because we have a lot more life experience from which to draw.

Believing you can fix your grandchild's problems or giving advice is often where a grandparent can fail. Too often it seems to become the expected or stereotyped role for a grandparent to give advice or criticism. But what if as a grandparent you could practice taking on the role of emotional support by refraining from passing judgment—and certainly refraining from saying something such as *well, in my day . . .*or, as Brown points out in her effective video for this topic on YouTube, refrain from using the words, *at least*, because, as she points out, empathy rarely starts with the words, *at least*. Like, *at least you don't have it as bad as I did at your age!* Or *at least your life is easier than . . .* Oftentimes the best response is, *I don't know what to say, but I am really glad you told me*. Or, *I don't know what to say, but I'm here to listen whenever you just want to talk* (Brown, 2013).

Fixing your grandchild's problem is not often what is needed from your role as grandparent, and often it is not within your ability to do so. Sharing a listening, caring ear is something you can provide. You might become a catalyst to showing your grandchildren by example what it means to show empathy, a character quality sometimes lacking in our world these days. When you create a space in which your grandchild can feel heard, cared about, and understood, and also feel loved and accepted unconditionally, you are in a position to build bridges and plant seeds.

BUILDING BRIDGES, PLANTING SEEDS

Thriving in a culture obsessed with fear of the other

I learned that courage was not the absence of fear, but the triumph over it. The brave man is not he who does not feel afraid, but he who conquers that fear. —Nelson Mandela

---

When I was in full-time family ministry, our congregation partnered with a community just south of the Mexico border in the city of Tecatè. We built houses, had monthly birthday parties at a local orphanage, did some tutoring, played games, and generally created a neighborly bond with many of the people living in that community. Many of our church families, even those with young children, went back again and again; however, there were also many parents in our congregation who hesitated out of fear of taking their children across the border. Would they be kidnapped by drug dealers? Shot? Exposed to illness? I watched a lot of kids who might have benefited from the experience denied it by overprotective and fearful parents, and sometimes fearful grandparents. They missed the opportunity of serving others and the opportunity for embracing cultural awareness. I am convinced that much of the fear of immigrants and other races is because we have never been exposed to other cultural interaction and thus perpetuate that fear in our children and grandchildren.

In 2006, a doctoral student at the University of Texas, Austin, Brigitte Vittrup, conducted a study with about a hundred families that became the basis for her dissertation. All subjects in the study were Caucasian with a child between five and seven years of age. The goal of that study was to learn if typical children's videos with multicultural story lines actually had any beneficial effect on children's racial attitudes. Vittrup began with a test for Racial Attitude Measure that was designed by one of her mentors at the university, Rebecca Bigler. Using the following measure, Vittrup asked each child a series of questions. For example:

How many White people are nice?
(Almost all) (A lot) (Some) (Not many) (None)

How many Black people are nice?
(Almost all) (A lot) (Some) (Not many) (None)

The descriptive adjective "nice" was replaced with over twenty other adjectives such as: "Dishonest"; "Pretty"; "Curious"; and "Snobby." For children too shy to answer, they could point to a picture that corresponded to each of the possible answers.

Vittrup sent a third of the family homes with typical multiculturally themed videos for a week. The videos included—but were not limited to—an episode of *Sesame Street* where the characters visit an African American family's home, and an episode of *Little Bill* where the entire neighborhood comes together to clean the local park. The next third was sent home with the same videos; however, this time Vittrup instructed the parents to use the videos as the jumping-off point for conversations about interracial friendship. She also provided the parents with a checklist of points to make, echoing the theme of the videos. The final third were also given the checklist of points but this time, no videos. These parents were supposed to bring up racial equality on their own, every night for five nights. The parents were asked to say things like:

- Some people on TV or at school have different skin color than us.
- White children and Black children and Mexican children often like the same things even though they come from different backgrounds. They are still good people and you can be their friend.
- If a child of a different skin color lived in our neighborhood, would you like to be his/her friend?

The first thing that Vittrup found interesting is that five of the families in the last group abruptly quit the study. Vittrup was told by two families that they did not wish to have such conversations with their children, saying that they felt uncomfortable pointing out skin color. The three other families declined to say why they decided to leave the study.

The avoidance of talking about race with their children was something that Vittrup noticed from a preliminary test of parents' attitudes about race. It is interesting to note that the test was of families living in such a liberal city as Austin where most every parent welcomed multiculturalism and embraced diversity. What Vittrup found of interest was that although parents may have asserted vague principles in their home—such as *everybody is equal* or *God made all of us* or *under the skin, we're all the same*—it appeared they had almost never actually called attention to racial differences. Basically, they all appeared to desire raising their children color blind; however, Vittrup could also see from her first test of the children that they were not color blind at all. More disturbingly, Vittrup had also asked all the children this question, *Do your parents like Black people?* In other words, if these White parents never talked about race explicitly, did the children know that their parents like Black people? Fourteen percent said outright, *No, my parents don't like black people,* while 38 percent of the children answered, *I don't know.* In this supposed race-free vacuum being created by parents, children were left to come to their own conclusions, many of which would be abhorrent to their parents.

As Vittrup expected, the results for the families who had watched the videos without any parental reinforcement and conversation led to no improvement over their scores from the week before. The message of multicultural harmony—seemingly so apparent in the videos—had affected the children not at all. But the surprise came from the other two groups of children (whose parents talked to them about interracial friendship) when she crunched the numbers and discovered their racial attitudes had not changed. At first glance, the study appeared to be a failure.

When Vittrup consulted her mentor at the university, Bigler suggested that perhaps there was something interesting to discover as to *why* the study had no effect.

Looking back over the parents' study diaries, Vittrup noticed an aberration. When she'd given the parents the checklist of race topics to discuss with their children, she had also asked them to record whether this had been a meaningful interaction. Almost all the parents reported that they had simply mentioned the checklist topics in passing. Many, it appeared, just couldn't talk about race and merely reverted to the vague "Everybody's equal" phrasing. "A lot of parents came to me afterwards and admitted they just didn't know what to say to their kids, and they didn't want the wrong thing coming out of the mouth of their kids" (Bronson and Merryman, 2009, 47–52; Vittrup, 2010, 192–214).

This study goes on to explore other research on *why white parents don't talk about race* and if you'd like to read more, I refer you to Bronson and Merryman's book, chapter three. However, the point I am making here is that many grandparents hold a unique position for having such conversations and telling grandchildren stories from their own experiences regarding such seemingly uncomfortable situations. This has the potential of being a strong area of influence that grandparents might fulfill where parents shy away.

For me, that's an easy one. I grew up to age seven living on a cotton farm in the delta of Mississippi. My parents ran the farm and my father also taught at the local high school. It was not until his health concerns caused his doctor to give him an ultimatum that he would have to either give up the farm or stop teaching. The farm lost. But while living on that farm, my earliest memories were of playing in the fields and exploring the surrounding woods with the Black children of my parent's sharecroppers. We did not see each other as White or Black—at least I didn't, and I wonder now if they saw my brother and me as the kids of their father's White boss? But I was aware that while my brother and I got on the big yellow school bus, driving us into town to attend school at the red brick school building, my farm friends—if they got to go to school at all—had to walk to an old one-room cabin to attend school. These are the sorts of stories that grandparents can tell that construct bridges, invite questions, and create space for empathy, compassion, and understanding. As a grandparent, or when I served as a children's pastor at a mostly White, upper-class church in Southern California, I dare not hide these stories of my own life experiences that the children desperately need to hear. I encourage you as grandparents to share your own stories of racial interactions, even those in which you did not make choices of which you are proud. Our stories of failure also hold powerful bridge building opportunities between us and our grandchildren.

When bridges collapse, and the soil seems too rocky for planting seeds

I suppose you might consider me to be one of the fortunate ones. Even though I live three-quarters of a continent away from my grandchildren, I am still in their lives. Our family is not untouched by divorce; our son was married for three years and then divorced. When the divorce was announced one of my first thoughts was to thank God there had been no children. From accounts and stories of friends I do know just how hard it is to have the deep desire to build bridges and plant seeds in the lives of grandchildren, and how hard it is to be denied that blessing whether through divorce or estrangement or death. I feel that pain of knowledge and helplessness. I also know this firsthand from nearly thirty years doing children and family ministry. I have counseled countless families going through the pain and disillusionment of families being torn apart.

In one case the mother went to prison and as I am writing this book, she is still incarcerated. Every time I correspond with her, she asks again for my prayers for her children and grandchildren. Sadly, at least one, maybe two of her children are also in prison. She may never be able to build bridges between them. Last year I encouraged Kimberly to write down her story. She did so a chapter at a time, which she sent to me. I edited and helped her self-publish a book about her life. It may never become a best-seller, but it served a greater purpose of gifting her life story to her children. She was able to give copies of her book to all three of her adult children. Maybe they will never read the book. Maybe they will never share the story with Kimberly's grandchildren, but hope springs eternal that this story will live on and have a power to gift meaning and belonging to her offspring. I share just a small portion of her book in the bridge after this chapter. It is a letter she wrote to her children. Perhaps her story will also live on and have a power to gift meaning to you, the reader of this book.

The other stories in the bridge that follows this chapter are from friends dealing with divorce and dealing with the challenges of separation from grandchildren, or, in one case, the challenges of adopting their grandchildren and finding themselves wholly responsible for raising and caring for three young lives. I pray their stories will touch your soul and encourage you if you are in a similar situation or know of others dealing with life challenges that make it difficult to remain hopeful and intentional.

Bridge 2: Disconnected Stories

*Personal stories from ordinary grandparents
about when bridges collapse, and seeds fall among the stones*

Broken Time (A Lament) . . . *by Mary Kauffman*

I see the lines of eternity in a family . . . our parents and ancestors are the eternal past; our children, the eternal now (as we will always care for and worry about them as our children, no matter their adult ages); our grandchildren, the eternal future.

But sometimes the future appears in danger of damage and brokenness when the grandchildren are part of the ongoing struggle of a bitter divorce. This is the case with B and D. The link with these two grandsons is fragile and at times heartbreaking.

BRIDGE 2: DISCONNECTED STORIES

- I watch their faces contort on some visits as they have been told ugly tales about their father's family.
- I watch their father, our son, struggle to say only the right thing and try very hard to make them happy on those infrequent visits with his own sons.
- I send birthday cards to the boys that are never acknowledged.
- I have five-year-old school photos of them that have never been replaced.
- I have had wrapped Christmas gifts left unopened on their scheduled Christmas Eve visit to our home because they were both suddenly *sick* and couldn't make it.
- Their cousins begin to forget that anyone is missing at family celebrations.

My last encounter with B and D was at a restaurant breakfast near their mother's home as I accompanied my son on a visit. I could feel their father's anxiety to say all the right things, to be enthusiastic and joyful, to make the visit pleasant and right in the face of the boys' stiffness and lack of eye contact when we first sat at our table. The younger boy said very little and focused on his pancakes; his one interaction was when I told him a silly joke and got a laugh from him. The older boy gradually warmed up; he relaxed a bit when we asked him about sports. I learned that he is an avid basketball fan and follows baseball, too; he could talk at length and with great enthusiasm about different players and specific games. I realized that I, who am ignorant about almost anything athletic, had a chance to make a connection with this grandson if I began to read the sports pages in the newspaper; this would be a way to build a bridge. I felt the stirrings of hope that it would be possible to connect at a level that avoided any emotional difficulties, any choosing of sides. Perhaps we could take the boys to a baseball game . . . perhaps then we could have some easy, enjoyable time together that would make them comfortable with their father's family.

The next week I found out that their mother was petitioning the court to move the boys; she had gotten a good job in another state and felt she could make a better life there for them and herself.

My hopes of bridge-building evaporated. We would probably see them perhaps twice a year, while they visited their father for an extended (and hopefully pleasant) vacation. We would become the vacation family. I apologize that this is not a very developed story, but with the children of divorce, some of us have a relationship with them that is only a disjointed anecdote, as above, rather than a flowing narrative. There is a reason our God does not treat divorce lightly; at times it is necessary, but it has both a horizontal and vertical effect on families, moving across and through many relationships beyond the nuclear family. My hope is that with maturity B and D will want the full story of their past and work to build a narrative for the future, but our present time with them will be lost and cannot be regained.

A letter to my offspring from my prison cell
... by Kimberly Phillips

My amazing kids are Katrina, Kristina, and Kurtus. I so dearly love them and am hoping for a second chance to be there for them and to be the mom they have never had as well as be a grandma to my grandchildren. I truly am sorry for putting my children through my selfishness and taking all my childhood trauma out on them. I will hold myself accountable for my life. This journey I have chosen is all my fault—I blame only myself.

What I am going to tell you now is very humbling; however, I was awakened in the middle of the night by God and He put on my heart to talk about how special my kids really are. My Katrina, Kristine, and Kurtus are so amazing, they deserve the best in this world. I am going to finally be able to sit and listen to their hearts, cry with them, laugh with them and just sit and let them be them. I will be able to give them good advice and be healthy enough to communicate with them as well as help make wise choices through our various difficulties. My kids deserve a changed and healthy mother and that is what I am today, a healthy person. I have worked on myself to become extraordinary and they deserve this more than I can truly explain. I hope and pray for our restoration.

God says in His word that He would restore all the years the locusts have taken from us. He says in His word, *I will restore to you the years that the swarming locust has eaten, the hopper, the destroyer, and the cutter, my great*

BRIDGE 2: DISCONNECTED STORIES

army, which I sent among you (Joel 2:25). Did God say which He sent among us? Yes. He allowed us to go through the trials over and over, losing our material goods, friendships, family until we could get it right. God is finally going to give me this all back because of His grace and mercy first and foremost, then as well as my obedience to Him and dedication to do His will and surrendering my old behavior and being accountable for what I did wrong to my kids, grandkids, my family, and the community. I hope and pray someday my children will forgive me as well as the community.

My first born, Katrina, has always been a loving, caring, funny, amazing person. She loved to cuddle up with me and tell me, *Mommy, I love you*. She was one of my parents' favorite grandchildren. They spoiled her rotten! My dad always played with her and whenever my parents took her home they would always go really slow in the country so she could see the cows and horses. She absolutely loved that time with them. I love her dearly and look forward to renewing our relationship and being the mother/daughter set that God intended us to be, as well as a grandparent to her children and being able to form a relationship with them.

Kristina, my middle child, was in and out of my life because of my issues. When she was in my life, she was playful and rambunctious. Like her sister, Katrina, she loved to give hugs and cuddle. She loved to clog and still does to this day. She is absolutely phenomenal in the form of dancing that she has chosen. She is beautiful and looks as if she should be in the modeling industry. I can hardly wait to spend time with her and my grandkids! I am so looking forward to being a mom to her and a grandma to her four beautiful children, my grandchildren.

Kurtus, my only son, was not in my life during his infancy and the majority of his childhood. Before my prison sentence, I would go to the home where he was being raised, to visit and work on some form of a parent/child relationship. His adoptive mother was an angel to me. She is an amazing woman of God who raised Kurtis and Kristina in the ways of God. She took care of them, raised them during my incarcerations. God put her in my life just for the purpose of keeping my babies safe while I was working on getting my life in order, as God wanted it, surrendering my all and putting God first in everything. Now that I have arrived at the spot where God wants me to be, I will finally get the chance to be the mom that they deserve and share God's love with them, as well as be a part of the lives of Kurtus's loving children.

I pray and think about them every day. There is not a moment that goes by where I don't think about them and pray for their salvation, safety, and future.

Mom loves you, Katrina, Kristina, and Kurtus and all my grandkids. I appreciate you as gifts from God and will be a responsible mother from here on out.

—Your Loving Mother and Grandmother, Kimberly

Diapers, dishes, and discipline . . . . *by Gram Gram and Grandpop Bustamante*

Children and grandchildren are a gift from God and can bring both blessings and heartache to a family. I say this with experience from raising two beautiful sons that sadly became drug abusers.

In 2016 our youngest son died from an overdose. He was only twenty-six years old and left behind a four-year-old son, a two-year-old daughter, and a baby yet to be born in 2017. He battled for sobriety for years and was so sick at times that he wanted to die. And then he did.

The children's mother had her own drug addiction and could not care for them. She sent them away to a dysfunctional relative out of state in 2017. We went to court to bring them home and we won permanent guardianship in 2018. We hear nothing from their mother.

How could this happen? Why did this happen? Why did God allow this?

In spite of what happened, it appears that God had a plan that we didn't fully realize until months after our son's death. We believe with all our hearts that God took our son home to spare his children a life of pain and disappointment. We believe that our son's children would fall into a highly dysfunctional lifestyle and repeat these same life damaging habits in time.

My husband and I are not grandparents as much as we are parents all over again. Diapers, dishes, and discipline is the title of my journal! It's been hard but we know the kids are where they need to be. But we have doubts as you can imagine: ... have we learned from our mistakes? ... can we do this again at our age? ... can God truly trust us with their little lives? We don't have the answers to these questions, but we know that God is in control and with His help we can do this.

We also know that we are not alone. We share a story with many other grandparents who are raising their grandkids due to the drug epidemic that is redefining the definition of what a family looks like.

Our lives are loud, messy, chaotic, expensive, and all-consuming ... but we are committed for as long as God gives us breath.

Thank you for allowing us to share our story. Gram Gram & Grandpop Bustamante

P.s. Our oldest son is now sober and a fantastic father to a nine-month-old baby girl! Praise God!

I Miss Her, I Love Her, I Want Her to Be in My Life ... *by Sally A.*

I've been blessed to be a grandmother now for eight and one-half years. I'm the mother of four and grandmother to ten, ages one to eight and one-half. There're six boys and four girls. My three oldest children each have three children of their own. My youngest son has one daughter.

It's this granddaughter, Ann, who I will share with you. My other nine grandchildren all live in two-parent, loving and supportive homes, with all the stability and nurture that every child needs.

Ann is five and one-half years old. I have known her since she was just over two years old. Her father, my son, suffers from bipolar disorder that was diagnosed when he was in college. He had been student body president, captain of the water polo team, and an overall leader and achiever. After a year out of college, he was able to return, graduate, and hold a responsible job.

At age twenty-five, he suffered a traumatic brain injury in a snowboarding accident. His injury was severe. He was in a coma for nearly a week. He was hospitalized and then in an outpatient brain injury program for many months. The damage was in the frontal lobe area affecting *executive functioning* areas of the brain. Twelve years later he is unable to work and struggles with multiple effects of this injury. One of these issues is the acceptance of his new self.

Nearly six years ago, during an acute state of mania, my son met and was in a short relationship with a woman. They conceived a child. He was overwhelmed and not happy about this. He knew he could not be a parent, could not support a child, and could not emotionally deal with this. He and the mother split and he went into a severe depression that lasted for the next few years. The woman, who has a history of substance abuse, committed a felony during her pregnancy and my granddaughter was born while she was incarcerated. She was in two different foster care homes until almost the age of two, when her mother gained custody.

She reached out to me soon after Ann's second birthday. We met, I listened to her story and met my granddaughter, who is the exact image of my son. I fell in love the moment we met. This began monthly weekend visits, where I would have her and she would spend the weekend with me. I introduced her to her aunts, uncles, and other cousins. They are all very accepting of her as a member of our family. For emotional and psychological reasons, my son has chosen to have no relationship with his daughter. He does not see her at all.

I adore this child. We have formed a strong bond. We have such fun together. She loves being with her cousins, six of whom live out of state. I was thankful to be able to support her going to a Christian preschool, where she was formally introduced to God's love for her. We attend Sunday school when she's with me and say special prayers and sing about Jesus whenever we are together. I've been able to provide swimming lessons, ballet, and gymnastics for her. All a joy.

BRIDGE 2: DISCONNECTED STORIES

Unfortunately, her mother's addictions continue. Ann was back in foster care as a four-year-old for a few months. From March 2019 until January 2020 she was again in foster placement. I've needed to learn about Child Protective Services, the Juvenile Court system, Social Workers, CASA volunteers, court appointed attorneys, etc etc . . . none of it is attractive. None of it is what anyone would want for their grandchild.

Throughout this all, I continue to strive to maintain a relationship with my granddaughter. My highest priority is for her to learn of God's love for her. I see this as my role in her life. As she grows, she will have many challenging realities to learn about the two people who created her. She is now attending a public kindergarten and there have been difficulties with me having her for the weekends to continue attending Sunday school as we have done for nearly three years.

I pray for her daily. I have become extremely close with her foster family and we communicate via FaceTime and US Mail. She loves receiving mail; learning to read and write has been a great motivator. We send mail to each other.

She was just returned to her mother this past week. She needed to change kindergartens and make new friends once again. Ann has expressed concern and being frightened and sad that her mommy will return to drinking.

I've had to learn and accept that grandparents do not have rights. Grandparents see and spend time with their grandchildren at the pleasure of the parent(s). I have love and time to offer my granddaughter. I offer her being a part of a large family who wants to love and accept her. Dealing with a mother who is currently keeping me from her is beyond painful and frustrating.

As I had to turn my son over to the Lord, I must continue to know that God is also protecting my granddaughter and keeping her safe in His care.

I miss her. I love her. I want to be in her life.

Ideas for strengthening your internal family culture

Remember to tell your family stories!

No matter how insignificant they might seem, sharing stories of everyday family experiences creates stronger bridges between the islands that are our lives.

Reframe your praise and encouragements to your kids and grandkids.

Instead of *Wow! You are so talented!* or *You look beautiful in that princess dress!* incorporate questions instead, such as: *How did you feel when you were painting that picture? Did it turn out the way you wanted it, or did you surprise yourself?* or *Why do you think you played so well on the field today? You must have been practicing a lot!* or *Do you think it would be fun or hard to be a real princess? . . . Why?*

Be intentional about your family rituals and traditions.

Think of what you do that creates meaning in your lives together. Perhaps how you set the table and serve special meals. Or, how you celebrate special holidays. (Consider adding special holidays to your family traditions such as: your grandchildren's baptism-remembrance days or how you celebrate special firsts in grandkid's lives.) Perhaps being more intentional about sitting in worship together each Sunday and helping your grandchild begin to understand and appreciate what is happening in that space.*

*The Story of Sitting with Lindsey~ Lindsey asked to sit with me again. It's always so gratifying when she does that. I know what it means to me, but

BRIDGE 2: DISCONNECTED STORIES

what does she get out of it? Lindsey knows the Order of Worship inside out—up to [the Children's Message], when she leaves for Sunday school. She knows whatever is memorizable, and she feels the importance of playing her part in the worship service. Once when the pastor was giving the Assurance of Pardon I heard her start to speak, and then stop. Anxious not to miss saying the response but not yet quite sure of her cue, she began to say, *In Jesus Christ we are forgiven*, whenever the pastor would pause for breath. Now she confidently waits for *friends, believe the good news* before she draws a deep breath and sails into her part.

Lindsey can't read, but she mumbles along on the written responses and holds her half of my hymnal while humming along on the hymns. Our favorite is "All Creatures of Our God and King"—there are so many Alleluias to belt out. The fact that every now and then and *O Sing Ye* sneaks in where you'd expect an Alleluia only adds spice to the endeavor.

Knowing what's expected during the Passing of the Peace, Lindsey politely smiles and shakes hands with all the elderly (over twenty-five) people sitting around us. After a decent interval of this, we sit down again and tickle each other in a friendly way until the ministers return to their places—which actually is a very effective and appropriate way to pass the peace. (We know some adults who should try it.)

Lindsey and I always look up the Old Testament reading in the pew Bible. We do this because she so much enjoys being in charge of lifting it out of the rack and also because she is so impressed that I can find the place without a page number. We both feel more holy when we look up the reading.

Lindsey doesn't understand a tenth of what happens while she's in church. I, on the other hand, understand it on a much deeper level because I find myself looking for the meaning and framing explanations that she would understand. She never hears these explanations—we both have a highly developed sense of appropriate behavior. It is not appropriate to talk during the service, and after the service is when you play tag in the [courtyard].

After *The Time with Our Children*—when Lindsey leaves—I find the rest of the service flat. It seems to me it would be much better to have *The Time with Our Children* later in the service—say, after the sermon. As it is, even the

Presentation of Tithes and Offerings lacks zest because there's no little girl beside me anxiously waiting for the plate with a quarter clutched in her hand.

I feel sorry for people who don't get to sit with Lindsey even for a short time. Have they ever counted off the number of Alleluias in "All Creatures of Our God and King"? Do they watch for the wooden flaps over the organ pipes to move when Mrs. Talevich starts the *Gloria Patri*? Does anyone ever tickle them during the Passing of the Peace? Tomorrow is Sunday. I hope Lindsey will sit with me again.—by Ruth Rex Dorman, a member of First Presbyterian Church, Anaheim, CA. This story first appeared in the Presbytery of Los Ranchos newsletter, 1990.

Ideas for creating compassion in grandchildren

Invite your grandchildren to join you in special or everyday tasks which create compassion and resist fear.

We too often resist the invitation to bring our grandchildren along on compassionate missions such as visiting the sick or shut-in, or serving in the food pantry or homeless shelter; however, I encourage you . . . or perhaps I should say, I give you permission (you can blame me) to bring your grandchildren along. Sitting at the bedside of an elderly saint and praying for God's peace in their suffering can be a powerful means of engaging even young children. Perhaps helping to prepare a Thanksgiving meal and delivering it to someone in need. Going on a short-term mission project to help build houses in a poorer community or serving at an orphanage. As a grandparent, you might be just the person who could invite them along, and the potential for meaningful conversations in the car ride home are high.

Go on adventures into the wilds of your community —or outside your community.

Rather than driving everywhere, look for opportunities to walk with your grandchildren and take time to notice the treasures along the way. For example, I have driven through and around the community of Laguna Beach, CA many times; however, it was not until I was walking up Park Avenue that I discovered the fairy garden alongside the library. Finding hidden gardens and secret places and taking long walks on the beach with grandchildren creates connections and memories . . . remember that time when we _____?

Prayers for Disconnected Generations in the church and prayers for community

for those separated from their grandchildren~
(from Psalm 130:1-6, The Message)

Help, God—the bottom has fallen out of my life!
    Master, hear my cry for help!
Listen hard! Open your ears!
    Listen to my cries for mercy.
If you, God, kept records on wrongdoings,
    who would stand a chance?
As it turns out, forgiveness is your habit,
    and that's why you're worshiped.
I pray to God—my life a prayer—
    and wait for what he'll say and do.
My life's on the line before God, my Lord,
    waiting and watching till morning,
    waiting and watching till morning.

A prayer for generationally segregated churches~

O Lord, the Psalmist cries out:
One generation shall commend your works to another,
    and shall declare your mighty acts.
On the glorious splendor of your majesty,
    and on your wondrous works, I will meditate.

They shall speak of the might of your awesome deeds,
    and I will declare your greatness. (Psalm 145:4–5)
Lord, we know that we are responsible to tell your stories
    to each new generation
Yet too often in our churches we separate generations
    in our worship.
[You O Lord] established a testimony in Jacob
    and appointed a law in Israel,
which [You] commanded our fathers
    to teach to their children,
that the next generation might know them,
    the children yet unborn,
and arise and tell them to their children,
    so that they should set their hope in God
and not forget the works of God,
    but keep his commandments;
and that they should not be like their fathers,
    a stubborn and rebellious generation,
a generation whose heart was not steadfast,
    whose spirit was not faithful to God. (Psalm 78:5–8)
Lord, give us, as grandparents, the opportunities and grace
    to rise up and tell of your powerful deeds
    so that the next generation might know them
and arise and tell them to their children to set their hope in You
    and keep Your commandments. Amen.

A prayer for creating internal family culture~
(inspired from Joshua 24:15)

Heavenly Father, may all generations know of your goodness,
    your faithfulness.
Each family must decide whom they will worship,
    whom they will serve.
Each individual must decide whom they will serve.
The culture that forms our views of the world will step in and
    demand our worship if we do not make a decision to place
    You, O Lord, as first priority in our life choices.
Help us, as grandparents, practice encouraging but not
    demanding.
. . . practice modeling God-honoring choices but not forcing
    them on our grandchildren.
. . . practice praying without guilting.

. . . practice wise choices in our own individual lives without
    judgement.
. . . practice living by grace and not by shame.
As for me and my family, may we always declare that we will
    worship God. Lord, may it be so.

A prayer for cultivating compassion a world obsessed with fear of the other~

(inspired from Micah 6:8)

You have shown us, O God, what is good and what you
    require of us.
To seek justice, to love mercy, to walk humbly with You.
May we find occasions to model this requirement with
    our grandchildren.
Lord, it is not easy to practice compassion in a world
    consumed with fear,
We want to protect our grandchildren, wrap them in
    bubble-wrap, and keep them safe;
May we learn to trust and model trust for our grandchildren
May we experience mercy and kindness and invite our children
    to experience these with us.
May we see to walk humbly with You and with our grandchildren
    all the days of our lives.

A prayer for the times when bridges collapse, and the soil is too rocky for planting~

*(from Psalm 81:6–8 paraphrased and Serenity Prayer
by Reinhold Niebuhr)*

A voice I did not know said to me:
I freed your shoulder from the burden;
You called in distress and I delivered you.
I answered, concealed in the thunder.
Oh Lord, have mercy when I call to you.
Grant that I may be able to accept the things I cannot change
Able to change the things I can,
And grant wisdom, I pray, to know the difference. Amen.

3

Refocusing Our Priorities (Or How Not to Be a Consumer Grandparent)

Do not lay up for yourselves treasures on earth. —Matthew 6:21, 19

We buy things we do not want to impress people we do not like.
Stop trying to impress people with your clothes and impress them with your life.
Wherever you find the treasure, you will find the heart.
—Richard J. Foster, *Celebration of Discipline*

Treasure Seeking

I bring my gold parable box out of the garage and set up storytelling in the middle of the kitchen floor. I am not exactly sure why the hard travertine kitchen floor became our storytelling location.

This time the story was another kingdom parable, one about the treasure hidden in a field. At the end of telling the story—as we always do—we wondered together what that treasure *might really be* and how it was hidden. We wonder how this hidden treasure was like the kingdom of God and we wonder together why, when the people asked him to explain the kingdom, Jesus told this parable.

After our story was folded neatly back into the parable box, my granddaughter suggested it would be fun to go outside and dig for hidden treasure in our backyard. *Of course,* I responded, *only, how about we dig with our eyes and not with a shovel?*

Off we go into our very tiny and manicured backyard in search of treasure. And what did we find? Tiny flowers hidden among the blades of grass, and tiny insects that gave us lots to discuss about God's amazingly diverse creation. We found spider webs and lovely flat stones (I have a lot of ebenezers I've constructed in my flower beds—some very small and a few little larger piles of stones as a reminder of divine presence).

We looked at butterflies and birds that caused us to sit for a while by the fountain and watch to see if any hummingbirds might come and bathe in the bubbler. Turns out it was not exactly the time of day for hummingbirds to bathe and so I suggested my granddaughter come and wake me early in the morning and we would go down quietly into the backyard and watch for hummingbirds.

At about 6 AM, when the autotimer turns on the fountain, I woke to see two little eyes peering into my face from close bedside range. *Ah! Yes, now I remembered.* So, I poured my necessary-for-treasure-hunting cup of coffee and we sat oh so quietly and waited. It was a magical moment, probably moreso for me than for her, to sit quietly beside the fountain in the early summer morning while everyone else was still sleeping, watching and waiting for one of God's kingdom treasures, a tiny hummingbird, to appear. We were not disappointed. Several showed up. And we pondered anew the treasures of the kingdom hidden in a field, or in this case, a suburban backyard.

Where your treasure is

Do you sometimes feel so overwhelmed by stuff that it begins to feel more like burdens than treasures? I sometimes wonder if our stuff—the things we can buy—blurs the treasure that is the kingdom Jesus was talking about in this parable. And I begin to wonder just how many *real* treasures we might overlook in our obsession over manufactured treasures.

Even as I sit here at my desk writing on a Saturday afternoon, I look out my study window that faces our neighbor's garage and I am watching my neighbor—the father of six children—cleaning out his double car garage, a garage that has never, in my fourteen years living here, had a car parked in it—because it is filled to the rafters with stuff.

My neighbor makes piles of accumulated stuff, much of it made of brightly colored plastic, that he will take to the local resale shop and by next month the garage will again be so filled up that his ritual will start all over again. How do I know this? Because I also sit at my desk and watch the Amazon delivery truck stop by his home nearly every day with more and more boxes of stuff.

It is an interesting cultural condition that we North Americans are so delighted in possessions and activities that keep us entertained. In his little book, *The Attentive Life: Discerning God's Presence in All Things,* Leighton Ford quotes the nineteenh-century philosopher, Søren Kierkegaard, on the difference between our artificial, human-created accoutrements and the gifts of our creator . . .

> Displays of fireworks hold our attention with increasing levels of dazzlement. They start at a modest pace, then become louder, with more brilliant colors, going ever higher into the night sky, until with one final burst of noise and brilliance and color it is all over. The creators of firework shows have to produce more and more artificial excitement to keep us entertained. But with the stars in the heavens it is far different. We can, if we will, lie on our back on a hill gazing into the night sky, hour after hour, and always there is more to see in the unchanging canopy of the stars over head, more almost magical attraction, more sensing the mystery of the stars whose message in light was sent to us from millions of years past, more drawing of our souls to consider the vastness of eternity and the meaning of time. Silent stars are like messengers sent by the Creator who also created us, to lure us into pondering the meaning of it all and to consider the great end of our lives. Fireworks are like the diversions we create to keep us from facing the reality of our lives. (Kierkegaard, quoted in Ford, 2008, 114)

Is it possible for us grandparents to gift to our grandchildren the attentive life? The ability to pay attention to the created order of this world in such a way that the manufactured attractions of this world don't blind them to those silent stars, those messengers sent by the Creator who also created them?

The early church fathers named greed as one of the seven deadly sins. In his book *Seven Saving Graces: Living Above the Deadly Sins,* Steve DeNeff suggests that the alternative to greed is not so much depriving ourselves as it is placing ourselves in a position of seeking after something more satisfying. DeNeff submits that what we might seek after is the grace of hope and wonder.

Hope and wonder and those silent messengers sent by the Creator might be seen more clearly when we're not being obsessively greedy for more stuff, more experiences, more entertainment to hold our attention captive. Isn't this it? Isn't it this grace of hope and wonder that we so long to gift to our grandchildren?

Perhaps one reason why we North Americans always seem to be seeking after more stuff, more experiences, more entertainment to hold our attention is because in place of hope we live our lives in a constant state of fear, fear of losing our security, our control.

Fear is a powerful motivator for greed. As in another parable, we fill our barn with harvest and when it is full, we build bigger barns to hold it all (Luke 12:16–21). Watching my neighbor is my inspiration at this point. According to a self-storage industry report from March, 2020, there are between 44,547 and 60,024 (Harris, 2020) self-storage units in our nation (sources vary depending on definition and methodology) compared to only 13,837 McDonald's restaurants and 15,041 Starbucks stores in the US (Lock, 2020). In other words, there exist more self-storage units in the US than McDonald's and Starbucks put together! *You might want to think about investing in self-storage stock.* But in reality, this is simply an indicator of not only our over-consumption but also our need to place our security and our hope in how much we possess.

The bottom line is that our national value of consumerism has impacted us and especially our children and grandchildren in very real and diverse ways. For example, "since 1966 researchers at UCLA have been polling incoming freshmen across the country on a broad range of issues. In a fairly recent poll of university freshmen only two out of five said developing a 'meaningful philosophy of life' was a goal, while three out of four incoming college freshmen say that *to be very well off financially* is their essential [life] goal" (Ruskin, 2012).

Our possessions have become a kind of religion providing their owners with a temporary sense of meaning and security. We live in a hyper-consumer culture where we purchase happiness, transcendence, even community. "Consumerism equates to a constant dissatisfaction, a restlessness, a constant seeking to get ahead, and also a promise of freedom, status, even love" (Cavanaugh, 2008, 48).

All this makes me wonder how our relationships with our grandchildren are impacted by this cultural value of consumerism. Has consumption become the currency we spend in order to have our grandchildren want to spend time and love on us? Is it also the currency we are willing to spend in order to keep them from whining?

The Nag Factor

Boredom is one complaint the consumer world has no room for, and the consumer culture set out to eradicate it. A happy life, as defined by consumer culture, is life insured against boredom, life in which constantly something happens, something new, exciting, and exciting because new . . . not being bored—ever—is the norm of the consumer's life. —Zygmunt Bauman, Work, Consumerism, and the New Poor

I've found what makes children happy doesn't always prepare them to be courageous, engaged adults. —Brené Brown, Daring Greatly

---

Speaking of whining, "thousands of the brightest minds in the country," writes Gary Ruskin on mothering.com (2012), "devote their great talent, and use sophisticated psychological techniques, to influence parents [and grandparents] to purchase products, or rather to want products, regardless of whether or not they are good for our kids. These minds do not work to solve the nation's real problems; they work to create new problems for you."

Western Initiative Media Worldwide is a major market research firm that as early as 1998 turned over a large part of their research initiative to one of the largest markets in our nation: children. What has been termed the *nag factor* is explained by one of those brightest minds. Cheryl Idell, chief strategic officer for WIMW, says that the *nag factor* falls into two categories:

1. persistent nagging—the fall-on-the-floor kind
2. importance nagging—where a kid can talk about it

"Either," Idell says, "is a good first step, but not enough." Disney and numerous other corporations complete the job of getting kids to whine even better and give kids a specific reason to ask for their products. In other words, Idell's job is to make your life miserable. She even rates brands according to their *nag factor*—that is, their capacity to make your children (and grandchildren) badger you. Companies toil mightily to rate high on her list. Some of the most successful are McDonalds, Levi's, Discovery Zone, Burger King, Pizza Hut, and, of course, Disney. Like we couldn't have guessed.

James U. McNeal, a professor of marketing at Texas A&M is perhaps the foremost expert on selling to children and the elder statesman advocating a shift in thinking from viewing our children as trusting, impressionable humans that must be protected to seeing children "as economic resources to be mined." According to Ruskin (2012) McNeal sees the money in your kids [and grandkids], and helps corporations get access to it: His reply? "Children are the brightest star in the consumer constellation."

Also, while Europeans are at least trying to wage a more successful campaign to protect children, in the US the government protects corporate advertisers instead. Back in the 1980s the staff of the Federal Trade Commission (FTC) provided a long report on the vulnerabilities of children proposing a ban on advertising aimed at children. Our Congress, in response, prohibited the agency from issuing such rules and revoked many of the FTC's powers. Ruskin comments that because children cannot vote or make the large campaign contributions needed to win political power in Washington, and since they have neither powerful lobbyists nor are they a powerful political organization, the advertisers—who do have powerful lobbyists in Washington—win.

And not to hit us grandparents right between the eyes, but consumerism is not just for the young. It is a disturbing commentary on us of grandparenting age when we reduce old age to a bucket list of things/experiences a consumer wants to buy before we kick the bucket. With one finger pointing at you, I have three pointing back at me. Guilty. Or as Paul wrote to Timothy,

> Command those who are rich in this present world not to be arrogant nor to put their hope in wealth, which is so uncertain, but to put their hope in God, who richly provides us with everything for our enjoyment. Command them to do good, to be rich in good deeds, and to be generous and willing to share. In this way they will lay up treasure for themselves as a firm foundation for the coming age, so that they may take hold of the life that is truly life. (1 Timothy 6:17–19, NIRV)

The challenge here is to consider not only how we succumb so easily to the value of consumerism in our culture, but more germane to our topic, in what ways we might practice more intentionality with our grandchildren on this theme.

Widening our capacity for gratitude and thankfulness with children

> *Gratitude unlocks the fullness of life. It turns what we have into enough, and more. It turns denial into acceptance, chaos to order, confusion to clarity. It can turn a meal into a feast, a house into a home, a stranger into a friend. Gratitude makes sense of our past, brings peace for today, and creates a vision for tomorrow.* —Melody Beattie

---

You might want to Google "thankfulness and children" and if you do you will discover a plethora of articles on how to raise, model, or train children in gratitude and thankfulness. Raising thankful children is truly one of the most desired—yet difficult—tasks of parenting and grandparenting in our North American cultural context where basics and more are so easily accessible and where corporations pay big bucks to promote a sense of need and *nag factor* in all of us. If you do check the internet you will discover that most of what you read in all those articles to be worthwhile and potentially useful; however, as you might expect, they often consist of the usual suggestions such as practice counting your blessings, or a *how to* list of ideas for creating empathy and appreciation in your children.

Let's try a different perspective. I suggest that thankfulness might more effectively be seen as a *spiritual discipline* that enables us to model gratitude for and *with* our children. On the topic of gratitude and thankfulness, Henri Nouwen writes:

> Gratitude goes beyond the mine and thine and claims the truth that all of life is a pure gift. In the past I always thought of gratitude as a spontaneous response to the awareness of gifts received, but now I realize that gratitude can also be lived as a discipline. The discipline of gratitude is the explicit effort to acknowledge that all I am and have is given to me as a gift of love, a gift to be celebrated with joy. (Nouwen, 1994, 85)

The simple act of giving thanks has the potential of widening our capacity for discovering the sacred in our lives. The deeper and more intentional our gratitude, the greater our ability is to receive grace, that grace of hope and wonder that DeNeff (2010) wrote about. But how do we model this for children who rarely seem to have the capacity for contemplating their many blessings and recognizing grace in their lives?

It is a major error in culture today, even our Christian culture, to assume that children do not have that capacity for contemplation of the sacred. Surprisingly, when given the opportunity to participate in meaningful community, our children have a great capacity for worship. The practice of thankfulness, for us and for our children, might begin in worshiping together and partaking of the Lord's Supper in a multigenerational community of intentional grace-filled thankfulness, of which we may be reminded on a weekly basis.

Our children are watching us and observing how we model thankfulness in communal worship as well as in our daily lives. Holly Allen, professor of Family Science and Christian Ministries at Lipscomb University, tells this story shared by one of her college students as she was writing about spiritual markers of childhood:

> When I was ten, my mom had twin baby boys. Life was crazy for a long time, but when Scottie and Ross were six months old, my mom and I sat down together one morning and wrote a whole bunch of notes to people thanking them for how they had helped us ever since the boys came. My mom let me address the envelopes and put the stamps on. Sometimes my mom would stop writing and talk about how Mrs. Roberts had brought over like ten boxes of diapers, or the senior ladies class brought Sunday dinner for like three months. She kept crying; I didn't know what to think, but I knew it was important to write to everybody. (Allen, Espinoza, and Okholm, 2015, 3)

Creating intentional habits and practices

Small, yet intentionally named habits that we can model for our grandchildren have potential to instill contemplation and gratitude—especially when these habits are infused with meaning and maybe a little out-of-the-ordinary mystery and adventure. Things like handwriting notes through tears of gratitude, saying grace before meals, making a game of counting our blessings, a thank-you prayer at bedtime for the wonderful day, turning off radio, podcasts, videos, and music in the car and paying attention to the gifts we see right around us as we drive down the roads of life, serve as place-markers for the deeper gratitude our children will develop as they mature. The beauty of these intentional habits is that they are often much easier for grandparents to model and instill than for busy parents. For example, the story with which I began this chapter on seeking backyard treasures with my granddaughter was so much easier coming from me than it would have been from her parents.

The act of blessing our children and grandchildren also creates potential sacred space to reflect an attitude of thankfulness. The biblical text is filled with stories of people conveying God's blessing on others. One of my personal favorite stories of blessing comes from gathering our family and friends together before they leave home to pronounce a blessing on them. (You will find models for giving and receiving blessings in the bridge following chapter five.)

Another favorite story on instilling gratitude comes from a young mother in my church congregation who got an idea while changing her children's bed sheets and flipping mattresses. She invited her small children (then aged five, four, and two) to come into their rooms where she took permanent marker and wrote permanent prayers of thankfulness on the slats of their bed frames—even on the toddler's crib! These permanent marker prayers serve as a constant reminder of thankfulness and God's provision in their lives.

Another favorite story is also from that same family when the children were older. For Mom's birthday gift she requested the children spend a whole Saturday with her—in her honor and as their gift to her—walking the beach with her early in the morning before the crowds arrived, picking up trash on the shore; then off to the supermarket to pass out flowers to folks as they came out of the store; and finally packing sack lunches and going to a local park to pass out meals to homeless persons.

Wondering together

The act of asking open-ended *wondering questions* creates space for contemplation on biblical stories and space for reflecting on thankfulness in most any life situation. When we read biblical stories such as that of the ten lepers (Luke 17) and invite children to wonder why that one man came back to say thank you, or to wonder how it must have felt to be healed and know that you could again be accepted into community, we create space for our children to recognize the place of gratitude in their own lives. Or when we tell the story of the Lord's Supper we can wonder together what it would have been like to have been there to receive that bread and wine from the hands of Jesus. To wonder why we receive communion *together* in our church family and especially when we are remembering—or re-membering ourselves to—the Lord's Supper, we can wonder to ourselves about how we are intentionally inviting our grandchildren into an eternal community of thankfulness.

The practice of paying attention with grandchildren even when there is never enough time . . .

> *The real questions for parents [and grandparents] should be:* Are you engaged? Are you paying attention? *If so, plan to make lots of mistakes and bad decisions. Imperfect parenting moments turn into gifts as our children watch us try to figure out what went wrong and how we can do better next time. The mandate is not to be perfect and raise happy children. Perfection doesn't exist, and I've found what makes children happy doesn't always prepare them to be courageous, engaged adults.* —Brené Brown, Daring Greatly

---

In her book *An Altar in the World*, Barbara Brown Taylor tells the story of Moses turning aside from his task of driving sheep to pay attention to a bush. Taking a time out to encounter the burning bush allowed Moses the opportunity to discover God's purpose in his life. And even more than the issue of the *nag factor* and corporations marketing to our children, one of the biggest obstacles to living thankfully with our children in our world today is the issue of time. It seems as though there is never enough of it. Diverted by our rushed lives and needing to be entertained, how often do we miss the opportunities to be mindful of the blessings and the *burning bushes* along our path? Let alone the opportunity to share these with our children?

Looking for signs and wonders of God's creation and God's kingdom treasures, and taking time to pay attention to the world around us, has the potential to do more to counter greed and consumerism than we might imagine. (You can read more about searching for altars and paying attention in chapters six and seven of this book.) When we take time ourselves—as well as with our grandchildren—to discover tiny flowers blooming their hearts out among the blades of grass, to discover unusual designs on rocks or rocks stacked into *ebenezers*, or spider webs among the succulents, or when we take time to sit very still and wait for hummingbirds to come take a bath in the fountain (especially with grandchildren), the pay off has the potential to be really awe-inspiring. As with my granddaughter, it is especially hard for any four-year-old to sit very still and very quiet long enough for a hummingbird to feel unthreatened, but sure enough, the tiny bird showed up and rewarded our patience, thereby giving us the opportunity to experience awe and gratitude for God's gifts and time to consider together what God's kingdom might *really* mean.

Cultivating thankfulness begins with patience and a widening of our capacity to wait and watch for grace to appear. As parents, grandparents, and others who minister with children, it behooves us to cultivate the art of paying attention, a habit that is in short supply in our wired and active culture today. It is ever so much more valuable to instill gratitude and thankfulness than simply telling our children to say *please* and *thank you*. Opening our eyes to new and intentional ways of welcoming our grandchildren, blessing our grandchildren, nurturing them in gentleness, and coming alongside our grandchildren on their spiritual journeys has the potential for changing the way we, *and they,* see the world.

*Gratitude unlocks the fullness of life and turns what
we have into enough, and more.* —Melody Beattie

Bridge 3: Relational Consumption

Personal stories from ordinary grandparents and grandchildren on strategies for countering the cultural values of consumerism and entitlement

To Be a Grandmother and Great-grandmother
. . . by Toedy Gray

To be a grandmother to the toddler is different than being the grandmother of a teen and then an adult with children of their own. When I became a grandmother at age thirty-nine, I was full of energy and all I wanted was to take care of that baby boy. As he grew, I bought every toy, every bike, four-wheeler, and motorcycle on the market. He was rich with toys. His mother, my daughter, let me. She didn't have the money, and she put no restraint on me. I looked for ways to reward him for anything he did.

So be it, he associated me with things. I am sorry to say throughout his adult life he still came to me for anything he wanted, and he struggled at providing for himself. When I became a great-grandmother, I started the same routine. I started paying my seven-year-old great-grand to do house chores; however, her mom stopped it and told her she should never take pay for helping grandma.

I had to think of other ways to give her money and gifts. Her mother, my granddaughter, taught us both it was all about love and care for one another. So, my relationship is different with the great-granddaughter. I give her gifts throughout the year for no occasion except love. When she visits me, she loves to organize my house as a gift of love to me. I am so glad we started this tradition because she was very confused when her parents joined up with some people who do not celebrate Christmas or Easter. I could feel the hurt and disappointment when she called me and said she could not accept presents at Christmas or Easter. I assured her that we would all be okay because we give gifts all year for love for one another. Many times, as grandmothers and grandfathers, we have to go along with change to keep the love and peace in our family.

A Gift from my Grampy ... *by Robin Tuner*

My grampy read a handful of books throughout college with me. Over my years of college, he decided to order a book or two from my reading for the semester so he could keep a pulse on what I was learning. I had grown up around the corner from him, but he didn't start reading books from my courses until we were long distance, and it meant the world to me! My college friends also thought he was pretty cool. I think it would be even easier for a grandparent of a younger reader to join in the long-distance reading!

BRIDGE 3: RELATIONAL CONSUMPTION

Prayers for Simplicity and Balance

A Prayer for Realignment~

O Lord, may I learn to see my world through the lens
    of your kingdom purpose.
May I be an instrument of refocusing in the lives of
    my grandchildren.
Helping them, in fun and create ways, to desire less *stuff*
    and desire richer life experiences.

A Prayer for Widening Our Capacity to See~

Heavenly Father, widen my capacity to see the world
    through your eyes,
so that I desire simplicity in my life and encourage
    my grandchildren.
May I, O Lord, become the change I desire to see in the world.

A Prayer for Treasure Hunting~

Dear Lord, from your Word you remind me
    that *where my treasure is, there my heart will be also.*
And so, dear Lord,
I ask for strength of purpose to seek only treasures that honor you.
I ask for strength of purpose to encourage my grandchildren
    toward the treasures that are eternal.

A template for writing a mission statement (To create a clear, easy-to-follow vision for your life & legacy)

Work on this alone, with your family
or with an accountability partner

Step One—

How would I/we like to be remembered and what impact do I/we hope to have on our children (and our children's children)? On our church? On our community? On the world?

Step Two—

Make a list so you can explore what you or your family is all about:

- What three words define me/us?
- What is my/our *identity? Who am I? Who are we? What makes us tick?*
- How do I/we define a *successful* life/family?
- What is my/our *purpose* for being . . . for being married/for being family?
- What three things are truly important to me/us as a family?
- Why do we need each other/how do we support and encourage one another?
- In what ways are we stronger together than apart?
- What guiding principles do I/we want to model for our children/grandchildren to help them prepare for adulthood and to lead responsible, caring lives?
- Who are my/our heroes? What is it about them that we like and would like to emulate?
- What three traditions do we hope might be passed on to our children's families?
- What three traditions do we keep from our own family of origin?

BRIDGE 3: RELATIONAL CONSUMPTION

- What sort of traditions would we enjoy creating for our children/grandchildren?
- What does it mean for us to be part of God's kingdom? (individually/as a family)
- Can I/we identify our *spiritual gifts* and how we use them?

Step Three—*Write your Mission Statement*

Refine, distill, pull all the ideas together into some kind of expression that reflects your passions, your identity, your purpose, and your goals as a person/a family.

Note: the fewer words, the easier to remember! One sentence or a few bullet points work best.

Step Four—*Translate the mission into the fabric of daily life*

The actual writing is only the beginning. Keep this statement in a visible place in your home. It should carry the power and reminder of shared vision and values. It can help to keep you, your marriage, your family focused and together . . . even in the midst of life challenges! (Adapted from Stephen Covey, *The Seven Habits of Highly Effective Families*)

4

Creating Meaning and Moments of R.E.&A.L.

---

*Vincent van Gogh said, I long so much to make beautiful things.
But beautiful things require effort—and disappointment and perseverance.
Van Gogh understood the pain of being unfinished. He knew the time it took
to add the layers and depth on a canvas that creates something spectacular.
I suspect he understood that in some way, his work was never complete.
There will continually be layers added and places of light and darkness to explore.
There is tremendous pain, disappointment, and strained perseverance in that understanding.
And yet, like the time it takes to add layers to a painting, it is this precise thing that produces
the beauty we long for in the first place.* —Melissa Maimone (blog post, 10/29/2013)

One day in the nursery the Velveteen Rabbit asked the old Skin Horse about becoming real.

What is REAL? asked the rabbit . . .

Real isn't how you are made, said the Skin Horse. *It's a thing that happens to you. When a child loves you for a long, long time, not just to play with, but REALLY loves you, then you become REAL.*

Does it hurt? asked the rabbit.

Sometimes, said the Skin Horse, for he was always truthful. *When you are real you don't mind being hurt.*

Does it happen all at once, like being wound up, he asked, *or bit by bit.*

It doesn't happen all at once, said the Skin Horse. *You become. It takes a long time. That's why it doesn't often happen to people who break easily, or have sharp edges, or who have to be carefully*

> kept. Generally, by the time you are real, most of your hair has been rubbed off, and your eyes drop out and you get loose in the joints and very shabby. But these things don't matter at all, because once you're real you can't be ugly, except to people who don't understand.
>
> —Margery Williams, *The Velveteen Rabbit*

Becoming real by becoming R.E.&A.L
(Relationally Engaged & Always Listening)

My husband made an observation the other day. He was noticing how many women these days seem to be gluing on false eyelashes. I think he is right. I hadn't really noticed it much before but after that observation, he and I started a game of pointing it out when we see it. They are women on TV, women waiting on us behind the fast food counters, women at the gym, even the anchorwoman on network news. I started to write something snarky about it on my Facebook feed; however, as I began to write, I experienced a moment of self-reflection and asked myself, why am I bothered by this? Does it matter if someone glues on fake eyelashes? Or colors their hair purple or covers their body with tattoos? I began to wonder if I am guilty of equating being *real* with being *au naturel*? Does how one dresses or how much makeup, tattoos, fake eyelashes one uses or refuses to use really have anything to do with realness?

I have to be honest and say that I would be hard-pressed to consider many of my non-adorned friends to be more *real* than several of my heavily inked and jewelry-adorned friends. And even though the Skin Horse would have us believe that much loved toys or people only become real after "most of your hair has been rubbed off, and your eyes drop out and you get loose in the joints and very shabby"; and in spite of the fact that the *good* grandmother of fairytale fame is always very old, her face wrinkled, her hair like snow and her cheeks like cherries, while the wicked grandmother is almost always portrayed the opposite; what really makes us real for our grandkids remains somewhat arbitrary.

Still, I am pretty sure I agree with Margery Williams that becoming real takes a long time and it "doesn't often happen to people who break easily, or have sharp edges, or have to be carefully kept." And I should also add that becoming *real* is hard for people who are always looking to the next new best thing to give them meaning in life.

We usually think of *real* people as those willing to live outside the influences of mainstream culture; however, I suggest that what makes people real is not necessarily living outside mainstream culture but rather their ability to create a strong *internal* culture that defines them more than the outside or *external* culture in which they live. In other words, it doesn't mean that they shun culture but rather that their identity, their named traditions, rituals, and stories define them more than values of the surrounding culture. (This is a theme we explored in chapter two and one that we will discuss further in chapters six and seven.)

Real people are people we can sit beside on the proverbial—or real—front porch listening to their stories, feeling confident that they are willing and ready to sit beside us and listen to our stories too. They are people who are not only interesting to listen to, but equally important, they are interested in listening to us. In other words, to become a *real* person requires the ability to be R.E.&A.L. (relationally engaged & always listening).

I worry that too many grandparents of my generation, the boomers who came of age in the Woodstock and Vietnam War era, and the era in which the world of technology was and still is changing at breakneck speed, often find it hard to sit still and listen and harder still to take time to articulate our own stories. They are people that are adjusted more toward CPA (Continuous Partial Attention) and FOMO (Fear Of Missing Out)—conditions that define our current culture—than they are to being R.E.&A.L. (relationally engaged and always listening). Because of this they often find it harder to create that internal culture because they are so influenced by the surrounding culture acting on them. We of the boomer generation are often defined more by our shared cultural history, by the music we've listened to, the movies that influence us, the TV programs we grew up watching, the national crises we've encountered together, than we are defined by our family history, our family stories or even, for that matter, by our biblical family stories. After all, it was primarily in our generation that biblical stories became less about stories we belonged to and more about springboards for object lessons to shape our moral character. And you might even want to add that sometimes folks of our generation find ourselves more focused on avoidance tactics and lament than on the risk of opening our hearts and souls up to others. Those of us in the boomer generation are more privatized and individualistic than any generation that came before us. But perhaps not as much as the generations that are coming after us?

Much of what defines our new generation of grandparents is mobility, moving and traveling both for work and for pleasure more frequently than past generations. The family breakdown we see around us today is partially linked to mobility, but it is also linked to various other cultural values that have shifted since the mid-twentieth century when we were coming of age. For such reasons, divorce has been rampant in our generation and marriage has, to a large part, become deinstitutionalized (Cherlin, 2004). These rapid changes in culture often leave us feeling that we're spinning too fast and just trying to keep up.

A need for digging more wells and building fewer fences . . .

> *Never believe that a few caring people can't change the world.*
> *For, indeed, that's all who ever have.* —Margaret Mead

The old adage goes that nobody cares how much you know until they know how much you care. This is particularly true of adolescent and young adult aged grandchildren. Listening truly and deeply to grandkids is among the most important jobs of a grandparent. Grandkids will seldom listen to advice or even listen to your stories until they know how much you care. And, of course, one of the problems is that you may care greatly but still not be able to show it. How do grandparents earn the right to speak into the lives of grandchildren? I suspect that none of us wants the status of being *that* grandparent who holds no authority and lets the kids get away with anything. The balance comes in earning the right to speak the truth and then speak it in love.

In the early 1970s, developmental psychologist Diane Baumrind became well known for her theories on parenting styles. Through her studies Baumrind identified three initial parenting styles: authoritative parenting, authoritarian parenting, and permissive parenting. Although her research was primarily applied to parents, I believe that aspects of her research that have been extensively developed by others over the last half century also apply to understanding our role and responsibility as grandparents—though with a twist. This is where grandparents get to step back and at least partially get that do-over I mentioned in the introduction to this book.

Do-overs have to be carefully navigated. For example, I have observed very authoritarian parents, often fathers, who turn into permissive grandpas. In such cases there are few wins because your adult children are frustrated by your behavior while your grandchildren see you as a pushover. Although many older men want to be seen as the fun grandpa, the move from fun grandpa to R.E.&A.L. is hard to maneuver. In fact, I am inclined to wonder if indulgent grandparents of either gender ever reach *real* status.

Perhaps the most important move for either authoritarian or permissive parents to make when they become grandparents is the intentional move toward authoritative grandparenting. Much like the authoritative parent or authoritative teacher or boss, an authoritative grandparent is one who is able to generously communicate high standards while staying responsive and tender to the child's emotional and spiritual needs. This is just the do-over for which many of us long. Authoritative grandparents must practice the fine balance between keeping boundaries and creating a free-for-all. I recommend that they do this less by putting up fences and more by digging wells. The practice of digging wells certainly has a lot more to do with becoming R.E.&A.L. than the practice of building fences.

Sheila Pritchard tells the story of a visitor to an Australian outback cattle ranch being intrigued by the seemingly endless miles of farming country with no sign of any fences. The visitor asked a local rancher how he kept track of his cattle. The rancher replied, "Oh, that's no problem. Out here we dig wells instead of building fences." The implication, I hope, is obvious. There is no need to fence cattle in when they are highly motivated to stay within range of water, their most important source of life.

Authoritative-style grandparents are well-diggers who create a thirst for authenticity; and just like a divining rod, children and youth are drawn to them. Such grandparents are attuned and nurturing while also allowing autonomy and encouraging interdependence. They should be able to step back, assess the situation, and provide reasoning and guidance with grandchildren instead of offering rewards or condemnation. They should practice walking the tightrope between setting clear expectations on behavior while being careful not to undermine the role and expectations set by the parents. They should fine tune the art of positive discipleship instead of bribery or punitive, forceful measures. Most importantly, they earn rather than demand or coerce respect.

Search Institute is an organization that partners with other organizations to conduct and apply research that promotes positive youth development and advances equality. On their website they give a list of tried and proven ideas for promoting healthy relationships and stimulate thinking about how different people might become more intentional about building elements of a developmental relationship framework. This is a useful website for grandparents seeking to fine tune that art of positive discipleship with their grandchildren. Here are four suggestions from the Search Institute for meaningful ways to connect (or get R.E.&A.L.) with youth.

- Express care and pay attention: One way to connect intentionally with grandchildren is to express care by focusing on listening to grandchildren when they talk about things that matter to them. Put away your cell phone and pay attention to what they are saying. Follow up with your grandchild when you know they are going through something, rather than waiting for them to bring it up.

- Provide support: Another suggestion from Search Institute is for adults (aka grandparents) to seek practical solutions for problem solving. This does not mean, per quotes from Brené Brown in chapter one on creating empathy in children, that seeking solutions for problem solving means always being ready to give advice or pass judgment. That would be putting up fences rather than digging wells! Rather, this form of support means listening first and then, when necessary, being willing to model how to ask for help when it is needed. It may also mean shifting levels of support to give more when grandchildren are truly struggling and know when to step back as their skills and confidence build.

- Challenge growth: One idea for an intentional way for a grandparent to dig wells from which grandchildren may want to drink is to create spaces for them to share the things they look forward to or dream about and assist them to distill and highlight future goals. Challenge them to think differently by asking hard questions, providing alternate explanations, and encouraging them—and yourself—to be open to different opinions, thus building new skills and expanding their and your creative thinking skills. Practice the gift of emphasizing mistakes as necessary parts of learning and praise them for hard work, whether they succeed or fail!

- Share power: Another means of digging wells from which our grandchildren will want to drink is by inviting them to participate in decision making about activities you do together and what you talk about. The trick is not to jump too fast when they don't make quick decisions or be too quick to bring up new things to talk about. As I type this I may be pointing one finger at you; however, keep in mind that I am pointing three back at me! Both in grandparenting and in mentoring there are those times when I am too quick to keep the conversation going or the ideas flowing, and even as I am being too quick I am regretting not allowing more space for their input. When you can manage to do so, help young people think through options and choices. Whether it is deciding how to spend the day or deciding major life choices, ask questions such as *So, what could you do differently to tackle that problem?* Not rushing in to solve the challenges for them can make all the difference in their emotions as well as in your relationship with one another. Be intentional about learning from your grandchildren—and show it. Young people have a lot to teach adults. Let them know when you've learned something from them that you're excited about.

- Finally, Search Institute encourages you to consider how you might expand possibilities with your grandchildren. As you are able, seek out opportunities to connect your grandchildren with people and places that broaden their worldview. Introduce them to a wide range of people, places, ideas, cultures, and vocations. Begin with some that you are also curious about. When young people seem curious about an activity, topic, or issue, ask questions such as *What strikes you about this?* In the bridge following chapter five, my friend Robbie Castleman writes about their family adventures in her story, *Camp Nona & Pop-Pops: Adventure and Memory-Making.* She and her husband, Breck, give a beautiful example of expanding their grandchildren's worldview on their summer adventures by introducing them to people, places, ideas, cultures, and history. You may not be in a position to take your grandchildren on a summer road trip; however, I challenge you to imagine ways that you might dig wells they will feel comfortable, safe, and interested enough to want to drink from.

I admit this is not easy. It is not easy especially when navigating the parenting styles of our grandchildren's parents. A good place to start is to read this chapter together with your adult children in hopes that you might come to a partnership. There are so many reasons why this is difficult and sometimes impossible; however, trying out the intentionality of being authoritative with grandchildren, even with limited access to them, can reap huge benefits, especially for grandchildren.

A particularly good reason for grandparents making such efforts is thanks to greater longevity. Grandparenting now takes place over much longer periods of time than in the past decades (Uhlenberg, 1996). There has been an increase in the number of grandparents who have the potential of being actively engaged for two or more decades into the adult lifespan of their grandchildren. In many developed countries, approximately 80 percent of older persons are grandparents (Connidis, 2010).

Also, the combination of greater longevity combined with statistically lower fertility has given rise to what is referred to as "beanpole families," in which grandchildren often have more "vertical" but fewer "horizontal" family relationships (Arber and Timonen, 2012). From the grandchild's perspective, having one or more surviving grandparents, even well into adulthood, is becoming increasingly common. Three quarters of thirty-year-olds in the United States have at least one surviving grandparent (Uhlenberg and Kirby, 1998). Lower fertility rates translate into fewer grandchildren per surviving grandparent. The extended period of shared lifetime combined with a statistically smaller number of grandchildren create longer and potentially stronger bonds between the two "non-adjacent" generations (Connidis, 2010).

Therefore the rewards of being R.E.&A.L. with grandchildren are many. Add to that that today's grandparents are also on average healthier and wealthier than in the past, yielding more scope, in principle, for their active engagement with grandchildren.

Another important reward, especially with reports of adolescent and young adult suicide on the rise, is that adult grandchildren who have grown up with a closer and emotionally healthier relationship with their grandparents are less likely to have symptoms of depression than adults who don't have this kind of relationship (Moorman and Stokes, 2016). This holds true for the grandparents as well, who are also less likely to have depressive symptoms if they have close relationships with their grandchildren. In fact, research suggests that providing healthy connections with grandchildren on a regular and meaningful basis is related to longer life expectancy for the grandparent when compared to grandparents who don't spend quality time with their grandchildren or adults of the same age who aren't grandparents at all (Hilbrand, Coall, Gerstorf, and Hertwig, 2017).

Several researchers have suggested that the most advantageous way to raise children is by surrounding them with a system of caregivers—like grandparents—that provide the children—as well as the parents—with a balance of love and support. This type of system is called alloparenting and involves situations where several people are involved in caring for a child besides the child's biological parents (Hrdy, 2011). Research suggests that the higher the number of close and caring relationships one has, the better the person's health and wellbeing will be throughout life (e.g., Feeney and Collins, 2014). We will take a closer look at the implications of this system in the final chapter that addresses the grandparenting effect on non-biological grandchildren in our lives. The role of grandparents in twenty-first-century families is more multidimensional, complex, and dynamic than it has been in earlier periods in history (Arber and Timonen, 2012).

The time it takes to add layers produces beauty

Melissa Maimone's observation on the painting process of Vincent van Gogh, quoted at the start of this chapter, is a visual life lesson on parenting and on grandparenting. It takes time and patience to add layers to our lives and also to our grandchildren's lives, recognizing and exploring places of light and darkness. Maimone writes, "There is tremendous pain, disappointment, and strained perseverance in that understanding. And yet, like the time it takes to add layers to a painting, it is this precise thing that produces the beauty we long for in the first place" (Maimone, 2013). Perhaps *real* status shows up best in grandparents who have journeyed through places of light and darkness and emerged with wisdom and stories to tell. That should not discourage us but rather encourage us to reflect back and project forward. Too often, in the name of protecting our children or grandchildren, we are unwilling to share our stories of failure or disappointment; however, especially for adolescent and young adult grandchildren, those are the sorts of layers they desperately need to see in the grandparent figures in their lives, layers that parents usually cannot show. A willingness to be open and honest and let older grandchildren know that we have not always had our act together and a willingness to share what we might have learned along the journey can hold tremendous encouragement for them. Sharing our faith testimony with grandchildren, not in a forced or formal mode but at the right time and space can truly become a witness to their lives and to God's grace in their own situations.

Being R.E.&A.L. means a willingness to be honest and vulnerable at the right times and places; however, it doesn't mean working through our own issues with our children and grandchildren. There is a difference between showing our layers and airing our dirty laundry.

A beautiful example of being R.E.&A.L. with grandchildren is found in the stories in the bridge between this chapter and the next. The gift of a grandfather that is so genuinely interested in engaging his college-age grandchild that he committed to reading and discussing some of the books assigned in college classes creates new layers of connection and experience, conversation and learning for both grandparent and grandchild. Or the story of another grandparent who took up surfing so he and his granddaughter could go out early mornings before school to surf together. And a grandmother who learned about and even discovered an interest in football just so she and her grandsons could share an interest in the teams. From my own experience I invited my grands (both biological as well as grands-in-faith) to bake pies with me and get interested in sewing. One of my favorite pictures with my youngest granddaughter, when she was just five, is of us sitting together on the stool before the sewing machine, both looking intently and placing our hands carefully on the fabric as it moves under the presser foot. Another sweet memory is with the young woman I have mentored for years as she invited me to teach her to quilt. It is not as hard as you would think, even though such skills are no longer taught in school, and there is an innate desire in most of us to create things of beauty. Besides, all such interests, whether it is reading textbooks and discussing, sewing, baking, painting, gardening, supporting an interest in sports teams, surfing, camping, or back-packing create wonderful and meaningful opportunities for common interests and thus moments of R.E.&A.L.

On growing old and becoming R.E.&A.L.

'Tis a fearful thing to love what death can touch.
A fearful thing to love, to hope, to dream, to be—to be, and oh, to lose.
A thing for fools, this, and a holy thing, a holy thing to love.
For your life has lived in me, your laugh once lifted me, your word was gift to me.
To remember this brings painful joy. 'Tis a human thing, love,
a holy thing, to love what death has touched. —Judah Halevi

Growing old, becoming frail, and worse yet, needy, is a scary proposition that we all face much sooner than we anticipate. Especially those of us in the baby boomer generation don't care for the idea of being seen as elderly. Add to that the fear of having our grandchildren love us less as we get more needy and closer to the end of life. Yet there is a grace and privilege and a sense of *real* that comes with allowing our grandchildren to minister to us. I have not experienced this firsthand and every fiber of my being fights the possibility of needing assistance in any area of my life. I want to be in control and want to be the one to care for others, and yet, I wonder if there is a gift in letting go and allowing children and grandchildren to care for us. It is potentially through such a need as care-taking that we also become *real* for our family. As in the Halevi poem above, it is a "human thing, a holy thing, to love what death can touch." It is a gift of being loved and being human to know the reality of aging and death in a culture that wants to deny such things. We put our elderly away in assisted living homes. My mother-in-law and her husband thought they would spend their last years in a lovely assisted-living situation that my husband called a cruise ship that doesn't go anywhere! However, due to complications of Parkinson's, my mother-in-law needed more care than that particular home would provide. We moved her to a small senior care home that hospice recommended; however, with this move and her health rapidly declining, I became the primary caregiver and POA. During this time, I found myself consciously and repeatedly giving thanks to God for the privilege of walking through this end-of-life journey by her side. The words of Halevi's poem came often to mind. She was always a professional, being in the banking industry most of her life. She was fiercely independent and did not want to be in such a helpless situation; however, it was in that very position that, for the first time in nearly forty years as her daughter-in-law, she truly became *real* to me.

It is important to take a moment to point out a distinction between gifting our children and grandchildren with the opportunity to "love what death can touch" and playing the victim. Richard Rohr warns against *wound identity* and victimhood: "It has been acceptable for some time in America to remain *wound identified* (that is, using one's victimhood as one's identity, one's ticket to sympathy, and one's excuse for not serving), instead of using the wound to redeem the world, as we see in Jesus and many people who turn their wounds into sacred wounds that liberate both themselves and others, those who whine about parents and authority for too long invariably remain or become narcissists. Oprah [and now Ellen] would hardly have a TV show if she could not highlight these many amazing people who have turned their wounds into gifts for society" (Rohr, 2011, 34). Most of us have known such victims who hold their identity in their wounds, in their suffering, and expect and even demand the attention of their family as they become more narcissistic and selfish. Such people seldom become a gift to their children and grandchildren. Such people seldom become R.E.&A.L.

How we age with grace and vulnerability becomes a way of creating meaning and moments of R.E.&A.L. with our offspring. How we navigate our relationships, how we show our layers and tell our stories, how we dig proverbial wells and invite our grandchildren to drink deeply from the water of dignity and truth and example—these are the intentional practices of becoming R.E.&A.L. in their lives.

Bridge 4: Stories of Becoming R.E.&A.L.

Personal stories from ordinary grandparents on strategies for staying relationally engaged with the younger generation and stories about the challenges and victories of listening to our grandchildren

Conversation in the car . . . *by Phyllis Bratton*

In my opinion, one of the reasons for the existence of grandparents is to allow children to ask questions about things that are troubling them, but that they don't wish to discuss with their parents.

My older granddaughter, S, who is ten years old, recently returned from camp. Apparently, some of the children, both boys and girls, swore a great deal, and the response of the counselors was simply to ignore it. S was quite appalled, and as we drove from church to our favorite Chinese restaurant (other family members being in other cars), she asked me what some of the words meant.

What is the b-word? What is an a-hole? Not the sort of thing a grandmother wishes to have to explain to a child—or anyone, for that matter. Then came the nub of the matter. What does it mean when you say *damn you* to a person?

Me: Well, when people are damned, they go to hell. So when you say *damn you* to a person, you are saying, *I hope you go to hell*.

S (shocked): I would never want that for anyone.

Me: No, you didn't find Jesus saying that.

S: What is hell, really?

Me: I read something once that made a lot of sense to me. Heaven is being always in the presence of God, so that you are continually surrounded by love. Everything you do or that others do to you, is an act of love. I don't think that hell has anything to do with fire or physical pain or anything of that sort. It means that you are totally shut out from God, which means that you are totally shut out from love. Think about how you would feel if you had no love from your mother or father or your brother and sister or grandpa and me. Think how you would feel if nobody loved you and you loved nobody else.

S: I would hate that!

Me: Yes. That would be hell.

S: Well, I didn't say any of those things.

Me: I would hope not. Remember that it says in Scripture that we are supposed to be conformed to the image of Christ. That means that we are supposed to do what Jesus did. You didn't see him going around swearing at people. He always tried to show them love.

S: That's true.

I don't claim to have a lot of insight or even to be terribly interested in theology. But it's important to give children as honest an answer as you can, given their levels of understanding, and let them take it from there. Tiny bits of understanding can be incorporated into their lives this way.

Grief had overwhelmed me so completely
... by Carol Mermis

The clinically cold seat of the 747 I was sitting in felt like the frozen ice pack of my heart. I was seated between two men who were speaking over me to each other as my head hung low. I was headed from a short journey that never would run its full course, interrupted by one horrifying phone call. *Come Home!! MOM!! Zane has passed away.*

What? I screamed, this can't be real.

Shocked and numb, I boarded the plane needing to be with my daughter and family. My thoughts turned to God as the plane ran down the runway . . . WHERE ARE YOU?? God wouldn't possibly let this happen. It is some cruel joke being played out like a bad dream.

The man in the seat to my right asked me if he could help me. I turned to him with tears streaming down my cheeks and said, *I doubt that you can help me!* He said, *Please, let me help, I am a minister. I can pray.* I explained my situation and both men on either side of me began to pray. Finally, my *out-of-mind* felt a peace as we lifted toward the heavens.

The minister said to me, *You are sitting between two ministers. There are also five ministers in front of you, five ministers behind you and ten in the seats across from you.* They all prayed for me. I quickly remembered who my God was. God was with me. God would never leave me.

I safely returned home to a whirlwind of people coming and going at my daughter's home. The viewing and service came and went in a thick fog that pressed in on me from all sides like a blanket.

BRIDGE 4: STORIES OF BECOMING R.E.&A.L.

As a grandparent you never expect a grandchild to pass away. Zane, a delightful blue-eyed chubby towhead toddler, was my joy. I can smell his wisps of hair as I write this. My biggest concern was my daughter. She slept most of the time in the months that followed. She only cried when I would talk to her. At the time my daughter had a seven-year-old and also a six-month-old. Christmas was rapidly approaching. I was the one who went Christmas shopping for the other grandchildren that year.

I put my grief on hold for a year. I had to be courageous and strong for my daughter and family. I remember the first time I heard my daughter laugh, which came much later. My turn came to grieve. I took a staycation. I walked the beach listening to my wailing cry. I told no one but God. Tears are God's gift to us. Our holy water. They heal us as they flow.

I remember a quote from C. S. Lewis, *The death of a beloved one is like an amputation.* This quote describes best the way I was feeling. It has been six years since Zane has left us. My family continues on but we are changed. We help other families who have had a loss in whatever way we can.

To walk along a grieving family or friend is a privilege. A sacred place. There are some consistent truths about grief that can help you show kindness and love for those who walk this lonely road.

- Listen more than you speak
- Don't be afraid to visit
- Simply be there
- Follow up
- Pray

If your friend will let you into their pain, consider it an honor and treat it as such. You can and will make a difference.

Blessed are those who mourn, for they shall be comforted.—Matthew 5:4

Prayers for Conflicted Families, Growing Old, Death of Loved Ones, and Becoming *real* (and R.E.&A.L.)

A prayer for bodily presence~

Fleshly God, you greet us with bodily presence and thus
    make it impossible for us to control you.
We give thanks for our bodies, destined as they are to death.
Through them you give us life. Make us your resurrection body,
    that the world may know your Spirit. Amen.

—Stanley Hauerwas, *Prayers Plainly Spoken*

A prayer for neglected gifts~

The beauty of green leaf turning red,
    the brightness of a stranger's face,
the joy of a cat at play, the sheer wonder
    coming from the generosity of friends—
for all this and so much more we give you thanks,
    we praise you, gifting God.
Help us remember, however, that you have made us,
    through Jesus Christ, your thanksgiving sacrifice
    for a world that refuses to acknowledge its giftedness.
Let us rush again and again to your feast of the new age,
    where you provide the space and time for us to enjoy being
    your joy. Amen.

—Stanley Hauerwas, *Prayers Plainly Spoken*

A prayer for becoming *real* and R.E.&A.L.~

How long does it take, O Lord, to become real?
Why is the journey so steep and so long?
Why are there so many rocks and mud puddles along the way?

How many times do I need to turn back from a dead-end
    and start over again on this journey?
Lord, I want so much to be real in the eyes of my grandchildren.
Give me patience . . .
Give me hope . . .
Help me to see through your eternal eyes.
Stop me when I try to control the situation.
Turn me around when I talk too much and listen too little.
Give me ears to listen.
Give me eyes to see.
Give me a heart for empathy.
Give me a mind to learn all the new things my grandchildren
    want me to know about.
Give me patience . . . .
Give me hope . . . . .
Grant me a willing spirit and help me to always remember
    that what I have and what I can offer to my grandchildren
    is *enough*. Amen.

Thankfulness for layers in our lives and the lives of others~

Colorful and mysterious God, you paint each of us
    with unique colors and designs.
It seems to take so long and so many layers of paint
    to create us into *imago dei*.
We are like living paintings,
    never finished this side of heaven.
You continue adding layer upon layer.
Give us patience and grace to allow the paint to dry
    between the layers
so they are not muddled together, turning us gray and bland.

What a blessing it is to be able to see
    the layers in the lives of others and observe
    the evidence of your creativity.
For every layer in the lives of our grandchildren,
    give us eyes to see your design,
knowing that they are, each one, an unfinished work of art.
We may not like all the layers we see but help us to trust
    your work in their lives . . . and help them to see the layers

of your design in our grandparent lives.
May we become the image of your imagination,
   a blessing for our grandchildren to see.

A Prayer for Major Life Transitions~

Lord, help me now to unclutter my life,
   to organize myself in the direction of simplicity.
Lord, teach me to listen to my heart;
   teach me to welcome change, instead of fearing it.
Lord, I give you these stirrings inside me.
I give you my discontent. I give you my restlessness.
I give you my doubt. I give you my despair.
I give you all the longings I hold inside.
Help me to listen to these signs of change, of growth;
   help me to listen seriously and follow where they lead
   through the breathtaking empty space of an open door.

—Claiborne, Wilson-Hartgrove, Okoro, *Common Prayer*

A Prayer for Adopted Children & Grandchildren~

We give thanks to you, O Lord, with greatest reverence,
for the gift of your Son, Jesus Christ,
who blesses our world and all families who dwell on earth.

We give thanks that in Christ we are all adopted children of God,
We are brought into your divine redemption,
which now subsists in each embrace,
each extension of love,
each sacrament,
each kiss and act of service.

May the adoption of this beloved child *(name of adopted)*
   be blessed.
May we the family of this beloved child
   enjoy the presence of God as our lives are
   intertwined together,

may we see the signs of your presence
    amid any trials or darkness that come our way.

In Christ, the Son of God,
    there is neither adoptive nor natural parents and children,
we are all born again in the Spirit of God and made family to
    one another.

May this child and all members of this family
    be blessed by the mysterious presence, mercy, and grace
of belonging together as Father, Son, and Holy Spirit model for us
    in the mysterious union of the Trinity, one in three.

—adapted from Claiborne, Wilson-Hartgrove, Okoro,
    Common Prayer

A prayer for the souls of our children~

O Heavenly Father, I commend the souls of my children to thee.
Be thou their God and Father; and mercifully supply
    whatever is wanting in me through frailty or negligence.
Strengthen them to overcome the corruptions of the world,
    to resist all solicitations to evil, whether from within
    or without;
    and deliver them from the secret snares of the enemy.
Pour thy grace into their hearts, and confirm and multiply
In them the gifts of thy Holy Spirit, that they may daily grow
    in grace
and in knowledge of our Lord Jesus Christ; and so faithfully
    serving thee here,
may come to rejoice in thy presence hereafter. Through the
    same Christ our Lord. Amen.

—St. Augustine

Six Prayers on loving what death can touch~

1. Help us name our lives as gifts

Lord of death and life,
help us find our life in you so that we might be free from
    our fear of death.

Our deaths have died in the death of you Son so that, like him,
we might rise to life made perfect by your love.
Help us name our lives as gifts
    so we will not jealously try to ensure, through coercion
    and violence, the regard and envy of others.
For we fear without such notice we will not be, we will be dead.
Such a living is not joy, and we know we were created for joy
    and life.
Let us therefore learn to live as gifts so that others might rejoice
    in our existence. Amen.

—Stanley Hauerwas, *Prayers Plainly Spoken*

2. A Prayer for the Death of a Loved One

Lamb of God,
    you take away the sins of the world.
Have mercy on us.
Grant us peace.

For the unbearable toil of our sinful world,
    we plead for remission.
For the terror of absence from our beloved,
    we plead for your comfort.
For the scandalous presence of death in your creation,
    we plead for the resurrection.

Lamb of God,
    you take away the sins of the world.
Have mercy on us.
Grant us peace.
Come, Holy Spirit, and heal all that is broken in our lives, in our
    streets, and in our world.
In the name of the Father, and of the Son, and of the Holy Spirit.
    Amen.

—Claiborne, Wilson-Hartgrove, Okoro, *Common Prayer*

3. A Prayer for Healing

In the name of the Father, and of the Son, and of the Holy Spirit,
    we enjoin your divine mercies.
Lord, why do we suffer?
Why do we hurt?

Shall our only answer
    be the eternal abyss of the cosmos?
Shall our only answer be the whirlwind of unknowing
    which engulfed Job?
Why do the wicked flourish,
    while the righteous waste away?
I am left speechless, left with the words,
I will trust in you, my God.

God, we ask for the sending of your healing Spirit,
    who came to us through Jesus, as he breathed upon
    his disciples.
This Spirit gathered your people,
    to be warmed by the fire of divine presence.
By this warmth, may *(name of sick person)*
    be healed and taken into your care.

—Claiborne, Wilson-Hartgrove, Okoro, *Common Prayer*

4. A Prayer for When We Doubt

God, you are mysterious.
And I don't understand!

Why do people have to die?
It's so random.
One person is struck by lightning and another is not.
One dies in an accident and another survives.

God, you are hidden.
And I don't understand!

Why do some people suffer and others don't?
One person becomes sick and another gets better.
One is born weak and another is strong.

God, it doesn't seem fair.
But then I ask myself: What would be fair?

God, you have the world in your hands.
That's what they say.

I've thought about this for a long time.
I've thought about what we suffer in life.
Death.   We know that one day we will all die.
Pain.   Injuries happen, and they hurt.
Injustice. Not everyone is happy.
Guilt.   We all do things we shouldn't do.
War.   People kill others, instead of getting along.

God, you have the world in your hands.
Surely you could make it better.
I've thought about it,
and I ask you from the bottom of my heart:

Lord, please just stop the suffering!

—Martine Steinküler, *Prayers for Young Children*

5. *Prayer After a School Shooting*
Dear Lord. Why? We just keeping asking, why?
So many whys . . . .
Why are guns so easy to get, so easy to use?
Why do people want to hurt other people . . . especially people they don't even know?
Why is innocence taken from our grandchildren at such young ages?
In the ancient words of St. Francis of Assisi I pray for myself and for my grandchildren:
> Lord, make me an instrument of your peace
> Where there is hatred, let me sow love
> Where there is injury, pardon
> Where there is doubt, faith
> Where there is despair, hope
> Where there is darkness, light
> And where there is sadness, joy.

6. *The Woodland Hills School District in Pennsylvania released the following poem written by student Antwon Rose, who was fatally shot by police outside Pittsburgh on June 20, 2018*

> I am confused and afraid

BRIDGE 4: STORIES OF BECOMING R.E.&A.L.

I wonder what path I will take
I hear that there's only two ways out
I see mothers bury their sons
I want my mom to never feel that pain
I am confused and afraid

I pretend all is fine
I feel like I'm suffocating
I touch nothing so I believe all is fine
I worry that it isn't though
I cry no more
I am confused and afraid
I understand people believe I'm just a statistic
I say to them I'm different
I dream of life getting easier
I try my best to make my dream true
I hope that it does
I am confused and afraid.

5

Invitations to Go Further Up and Further In

What I have observed over the past twenty years has increased my sense of urgency about the need for spiritual practice among us. If we do not learn to honor and strengthen the inner life of spirit, all the external changes in the world cannot save us. New laws, regulations, and technological fixes are all susceptible to human corruption and self-interest. If we do not know ourselves as beings created to reflect the divine image, we will lose the immense opportunity for transformation God has offered us in the gift of life itself. And if the love of God embodied in Christ cannot turn us, how shall we be turned? . . . We are beginning to starve for values of enduring substance.
—Marjorie, J. Thompson, *Soul Feast*

The desperate need today is not for a greater number of intelligent people, or gifted people, but for deep people. —Richard J. Foster, *Celebration of Discipline*

I have come home at last! This is my real country! I belong here. This is the land I have been looking for all my life, though I never knew it till now . . . Come further up, come further in!
—C. S. Lewis, *The Last Battle*

Even though spiritual practices go back to the very earliest centuries of the Christian faith and are also rooted in most other ancient religions, for evangelicals there was a resurgence of the practices of spiritual disciplines in the late 1970s and beyond, primarily due to authors such as Richard Foster,

Dallas Willard, Marjorie Thompson, and Henri Nouwen. Many of us embraced such writers and disciplines as a means of bringing our hearts and minds into alignment with God's purposes. Some of us began attending spiritual retreats, *something that hitherto was more closely associated with the Catholic faith*. Often such retreats were attended by groups with times set aside for individual meditation and personal reflections, but many of us ventured into the realm of private and/or silent retreats. And although writers such as Foster put equal emphasis on the *outward* and *corporate* disciplines, for many in our individualist-saturated church culture, we learned to practice our disciplines in private as we sought a deeper personal connection with God. Such experiences of personal time away with God and in practice of disciplines such as meditation, prayer, fasting, and study are important means of changing and redirecting our spiritual lives and bringing us further up and further into God's kingdom purpose; however, it is important to remember that although Christianity is personal, it is not individual. And occasionally our connection with our grandchildren can be strengthened through intentionally living and practicing our spiritual disciplines *outwardly* in their view, a process that may feel rather awkward for many of us in our generation.

Lisa Miller, director of the Clinical Psychology Program at Columbia University, conducted research on children's brains which is presented in her book *The Spiritual Child: The New Science on Parenting for Health and Lifelong Thriving*. On the topic of teenage brains, Miller writes, "Wherever their spiritual yearnings lead them, teens find spiritual growth through the quest process. My concern is that so many adolescents aren't guided to the journey at all or aren't encouraged on their way" (Miller, 2016, 258). A uniquely precious role of a grandparent may be to serve as a guide for the journey of grandchildren, especially when they are teenagers with a tendency to reject such guidance from parents.

In this chapter we will consider the potential blessings of becoming more effective in our grandparenting opportunities as we look toward the outward and corporate spiritual disciplines that have great potential for connecting generations and having influence in the lives of our grandchildren. Along the way we will walk through such disciplines and consider how such influence might be created.

But first, let's begin with an invitation, a challenge, and a privilege.

THE GRAND-PARENTING EFFECT

An invitation to create and follow a CIQ & ROL

Very often a grandparent becomes [a] special spiritual partner even when the parents are healthy and functional and spiritually supportive. In our busy lives, so often it is a grandparent who sits and listens to a child's questions, welcomes a child's feelings, and has the long deep talks at the kitchen table. —Lisa Miller, The Spiritual Child

---

I served as a vocational formation facilitator at Fuller Seminary for several years. These were groups of graduate students, most preparing for church leadership roles, but who often worked full-time jobs and also had families. The vocational formation groups gave them an opportunity to connect with one another beyond the classroom, share their stories, their challenges of ministry, and most importantly connect over prayer, dialogue, and group spiritual direction. As a group leader, at each session I had the privilege of guiding them through such corporate as well as individual spiritual practices as *lectio divina* or the *examen* (see models in the bridge following this chapter). During the last session for each quarter as Vocational Formation facilitator it was also my responsibility to invite them to revise their CIQ and ROL (Central Integration Question and Rule Of Life). Fuller Seminary required that each student write these out and then revise and refine them on a regular basis as they went through their degree programs.

The central integration question (CIQ) was simply a revisiting and reevaluation of God's call on their life and ministry by asking themselves the following question and inviting them to share their responses with classmates: *At this point in your Christian journey, how do you envision your call to God's mission in the world?*

The CIQ is about an ongoing process and focused the student's attention on the reality that vocation (call) is not only about career or even ministry that gives us purpose and meaning, but about participating in God's mission in the world. Perhaps the most important word in the CIQ is the word *envision*. Asking them to consider at that particular point in time what picture, what vision, what metaphor or image comes to mind when considering their call to God's mission in the world?

The Rule of Life (ROL) required regularly revisiting the practices, future hope, commitment to rhythm, and accountability they committed to hold to in life and ministry, each building on the others. For example, if the practices were listed as prayer, listening, hospitality, and worship, then the future hope would require an explanation of the hope that will come from integrating each of the practices into one's life. The next step was to consider when and how these practices could become a natural expression of one's life in Christ on a daily/weekly/monthly routine. This, of course, would require the practices to become *disciplines of life*. Finally, each student was to invite people in their life to help them stay on track and hold them accountable.

The privileges of inviting grandchildren into a CIQ & ROL

You very well may be asking what all this has to do with grandparenting. Whether you might be a student required to choose practices and make an outward commitment to rhythm or whether you are an adult making this commitment on your own or in a covenant group, we usually default to asking others around our same age or older to hold us accountable. What might it look like to invite your grandchild to become your accountability partner to encourage you to keep your spiritual practices? Or, what might it look like to be in a position of having your adolescent, teenaged, or young adult ask to have you as their accountability partner?

Would you ever consider sitting down at a coffee shop with your adolescent or teen grandchild and having a frank conversation on developing a CIQ? Could you see yourself doing something as simple as inviting or challenging them to *envision* what picture, what vision, what metaphor or image comes to mind when considering their call to God's mission in the world? Of course, this won't happen without first laying intentional groundwork in your relationship. One must practice becoming R.E.&A.L. (see chapter four) before such discussions can take place.

Developing a Rule of Life is possible—and also vital—for our adolescent and older grandchildren to foster a life of holiness. As Lisa Miller is quoted above, "very often a grandparent becomes [a] special spiritual partner even when the parents are healthy and functional and spiritually supportive. In our busy lives, so often it is a grandparent who sits and listens to a child's questions, welcomes a child's feelings, and has the long deep talks at the kitchen table" (Miller, 2016, 80).

A Rule of Life is a simple written pattern of attitudes, behaviors, and practices that are regular and routine, intended to foster a life of holiness and godliness. We build our Rule of Life by reflecting on the practical steps we believe God is leading us to take to discipline our lives so that we will live in alignment with God's will—so that we may indeed be holy as God is holy (Leviticus 19:2; 1 Peter 1:16). As faithful grandparents who seek to follow our own ROL, we may have opportunities to model this for our grands and even find natural opportunities to encourage them in such practices. (See ideas in the bridge following this chapter.) And, although we may convince ourselves that our grandchildren are not interested, in reality, given the ever-shifting, post-Christendom culture in which they are growing up, such modeling and encouragement and accountability to set up and follow a ROL may be the foundational structure our grands are longing for, even if they are not able to verbalize this longing. They can see it and feel called to it when it is natural and inviting.

Precisely because our spiritual practices and disciplines have come to be largely individualized in our minds today and because many Christians have shied away from such practices altogether, it may feel out of place in relationships even with our family members. However, I ask you to consider what spiritual practices—given a chance—might look like when practiced as family and community.

Perhaps a more culturally accepted description might be to serve in the role of a *life coach* or *mentor* for someone younger—a grandchild or other young person in the church. It might help to keep in mind why some people, perhaps our grandchildren, are attracted to more culturally acceptable terms such as *life coaching* or *mentoring*. This can be especially true when your own children are not raising your grandchildren in an overtly Christian home. The same goal by a different name can help avoid scaring off young people who may be intimidated by more overt religiosity. The key is to have the attentive quality of presence—that becoming R.E.&A.L. quality we discussed in the previous chapter. Additionally, in a time when social isolation is contributing to the global mental health crisis, the focused listening that a spiritual director, an accountability partner, a life coach, a mentor, or just a plain ol' grandparent can provide is a rarity and can help spiritual seekers feel known. The old adage from St. Augustine, "our hearts are restless until they find their rest in God," is true in the culture all around us, which seeks to fill the hunger and thirst for prayer and God with other things.

It's important not to bang our grandchildren over the head with God, but to create that space in which they *might* recognize and name the truth of their religious experiences. Because our restless hearts seek meaning, most people have experiences of transcendence and the holy that our culture cannot or does not want to talk about. As a grandparent, simply being aware and creating spaces in which grandchildren can notice God's activity in the world, and in their lives, knowing that you are a safe person for them to talk about it can be an invitation to developing a CIQ and ROL.

The practices of living inside-out
(service, compassion, and solidarity)

Nothing disciplines the inordinate desires of the flesh like service, and nothing transforms the desires of the flesh like serving in hiddenness. The flesh whines against service but screams against hidden service. It strains and pulls for honor and recognition. It will devise subtle, religiously acceptable means to call attention to the service rendered. If we stoutly refuse to give in to this lust of the flesh, we crucify it. Every time we crucify the flesh, we crucify our pride and arrogance. —Richard J. Foster, *Celebration of Discipline*

My friends Robbie and Breck Castleman are a couple of my favorite role models of intentional grandparenting. You can read their story of *Camp Nona and Pop-pops* in the bridge following this chapter. The thing I love about their summer adventures with their grandchildren are the layers and serendipitously deeper R.E.&A.L. that come out of what started off as simply an opportunity to take their grands on a road trip while giving their parents a break. As the children grew older the road trips morphed from getting their grandkids in touch with nature to exploring their family history on the summer of *The Nona Nevada Trip*, followed by the opportunity to learn geography, history, and culture as the grands got to choose the location of their adventures.

Another layer was helping their grands accept the reality that the summer trip meant that birthday and Christmas gifts were minimal so as to allow more money for Camp Nona and Pop-pops. But the layer that resonated most deeply with my soul was the opportunity to create compassion in the hearts of their grands with adventures such as their *the good, the bad, and the really ugly* road trip as they toured Civil War sites, giving opportunity to discuss the realities of race relations and Christian faith along the journey.

There are grandparents who create an assembly line with their grands where they make PB&J sandwiches, pack sack lunches (including small notes of encouragement and written prayers), and then hop in the car or, better yet, on public transportation and sojourn into the city landscape to hand out the sack lunches to homeless living on the streets and in city parks. This is a simple intergenerational activity for churches to provide by inviting all generations—children, youth, and senior citizens—to work the assembly line side by side and then hop on the train to the city together.

On PBS NewsHour in May, 2016, anchor Judy Woodruff asked the question, "What can a five-year-old learn from a ninety-five-year-old? At Seattle's Providence Mount St. Vincent nursing home, that question is answered daily. You see, the Mount also houses a child care center of 125 tots. And the full cycle of life on display is magic."

Special correspondent Cat Wise reported on this in the PBS *Making the Grade* series.

> The opportunity for generations to engage with each other has become an example for states struggling to find ways to improve access to high quality pre-kindergarten and this unique approach taken by a preschool in Seattle, Washington gives children life lessons that go beyond the classroom while also providing unique blessings for seniors. . . . The preschool [is] housed in the senior care facility where these generations at both ends of the spectrum can share storytime, art classes, free play, or simply observation from the large, low windows where seniors in wheelchairs can pull up to the window bar and simply watch the children at play.

It also provides the opportunity for such sack lunch making assembly line, as I note above. These are not biological grandchildren; however, just putting these seniors and young children in a position to serve together in productive activity contributes to society.

There's the story of a grandfather who serves meals to homeless people every Saturday and takes his grands along because he wants them to learn respect and value all kinds of people and to practice their faith in action (Garland, 2012). Another story concerns a grandmother, when asked what she would like for her birthday from her kids, asked for a day of service together, which meant picking up trash in an early birthday morning walk on the beach, followed by planting spring flowers in a local school yard (after getting permission from the principal, of course), followed by passing out cut flowers to strangers outside a grocery store for no reason other than just to say, "Have a nice day."

When their Pops was preparing to climb Mt. Kilimanjaro to raise funds for digging clean water wells in Ethiopia through the work of

Lifewater International, our granddaughters joined the cause with a bake sale and water station on the sidewalk in their neighborhood. It presented a perfect and tangible opportunity to engage them in dialogue about helping others in need as well as appreciation for the clean water in their home. Perhaps as a grandparent you are not as ready as Pops to climb the tallest free-standing mountain on earth; however, the act of engaging your grandchildren in activities that produce compassion and their ability to serve others begins to change their worldview and brings focus to their—as well as your—developing CIQ and ROL.

What are your stories of modeling service, compassion, and solidarity with your grandchildren? We need to share these stories with others so as to encourage us all. When our grandparenting is more about service and compassion and opportunities for engaging our grandchildren in solidarity with others we are more in a position to resist the temptations talked about in chapter three, on how *not* to be a consumer grandparent.

The practices of imagination
(imaginative prayer and spiritual listening)

> *I had grown in paying attention to my own conversation with God. I was even getting pretty good at helping other adults pay attention to their life with God. But when it came to these kinds of conversations with my own children, I quickly reverted back to asking questions about belief in God, the Bible, and the cross.* —Jared Patrick Boyd, *Imaginative Prayer*

I was recently asked to write an endorsement for a new book by Lacy Finn Borgo titled *Spiritual Conversations with Children: Listening to God Together*. I have been a fan of Borgo for a couple of years now since listening to her speak on spiritual direction with children at the Children's Spirituality Summit in Nashville in June of 2018.

Borgo asks the question, *what is holy listening?* She gives us five guidelines to holy listening with children:

1. *Holy listening creates a place where children receive undivided attention as they express themselves about the experiences of their lives.*

2. *Holy listening is when a child has a soul friend—someone who helps children recognize and respond to the presence of God in their lives.*
3. *Holy listening is confidential. We will never reveal what your child says to anyone unless it is for his or her own protection. (As mandated by law.)*
4. *Holy listening is safe. We observe accepted practices that ensure the child's safety whenever he or she talks with us.*

Borgo is addressing guidelines for a spiritual director with children, such as she is; however, these guidelines go to the heart of your role as a grandparent. This is the role of a grandparent when that grandparent has proven him/herself to be someone who is trustworthy, someone who is R.E.&A.L. and someone who loves a child unconditionally.

When children have a listening companion who hears, acknowledges, and encourages their early experiences with God, it creates a spiritual footprint that shapes their lives. Borgo writes,

> When we are fully present and open to another, we will be changed. Indeed, as you listen to God with a child, the child will lead you into a fuller experience of God's love and acceptance. . . . With the Spirit as the true Listener, and the child as the center of attention, a Holy Listener becomes a soul friend with whom children can talk and share. A Holy Listener is present with undivided attention, as witness, as a child shares about his or her experiences. A Holy Listener also helps the child recognize and respond to the movement of God in every experience. Holy Listening can look like playing with toys, expression through art, and talking with God using various means. (Borgo, 2020, 145)

My friend Phyllis, whose story is in the bridge following chapter four, discovered that her car had become a serendipitous location for holy listening as her granddaughter felt free to ask questions she'd have been less willing to ask her parents.

I discovered that telling *worship and wonder* stories on my kitchen floor to be a beautiful way of holy listening as my grandchildren—as well as non-biological grands in my life—as we reflected on biblical stories with *wondering questions*, we all discovered space for imagination.

The ancient spiritual practice of *lectio divina* becomes a means of inviting grandchildren into the stories and lessons we read in the Bible as we read them aloud with one another. Traditionally, *lectio divina* has four separate steps: read, reflect, pray, and contemplate. First a passage of Scripture is read, then its meaning is reflected upon. This is followed by prayer and contemplation on the Word of God. There are passages from Scripture, especially from the Old Testament and the Gospels, that lend themselves to this practice. As with most spiritual disciplines these days, many of us see *lectio divina* as a personal practice; however, it lends itself beautifully to a partner or group practice. For example, it was when facilitating the practice of guided group *lectio divina* with the vocational formation groups at Fuller Seminary that I discovered the depth of the story of Jesus and the woman caught in the act of adultery (John 8:1–11).

After verbally guiding the students through the practice we had a time of sharing. I have done this practice with this passage during the academic section on forgiveness in personal as well as corporate settings. It often brings out deep conversation and, on one occasion, it created a space for a female seminary student to lament the abuse she had suffered as a child; and space for another who had suffered at the hands of a well-meaning congregation in which she was discouraged from developing her gifts of ministry. When Scripture is read aloud, even one-on-one with a grandchild, then reflected on and contemplated, even by means of *wondering questions*, it opens opportunities for grace and connection. For the above passage from John 8, one might wonder with whom one most identifies in the story or wonder what and whom one observes as they look around the story scene. One could wonder how it felt to have the religious leaders disrupt Jesus' teaching to test Jesus or wonder how Jesus felt when this happened. There are so many things to wonder about this story, and there are so many things to wonder about most of the stories and lessons from Scripture! Depending on the age of your grandchild, you can decide where to go and how deep to wonder. My grandchildren will tell you that I even wonder when telling regular stories or reading books aloud together. If you have young grandchildren, a sweet place to begin is with Sally Lloyd-Jones's *Jesus Storybook Bible*. Reading this book aloud and wondering together sets the stage for deeper conversations to come in future years.

Another rich resource for imaginative listening is in Jared Patrick Boyd's *Imaginative Prayer: A Yearlong Guide for Your Child's Spiritual Formation*. Boyd wrote this book from his own need as a pastor. As he says, "I was trying to think through how to reorient our kids' ministry toward nurturing a *connection with God* and teaching parents how to ask the right kinds of questions so that our efforts as a church and parent's efforts at home would reinforce each other" (Boyd, 2017, 17). And, of course, I have to include the efforts of grandparents in reinforcing such home and church partnerships!

Boyd's book follows six parts, each exploring a theological theme: God's love, loving others, forgiveness, Jesus as king, the good news of God, and the mission of God. Each of these parts is made up of seven sessions: six imaginative stories and one week for review. There are enough stories, built on themes, to last a full year with a few weeks off for vacations, etc. Each story includes guided questions to draw the child into greater connection and each also includes some meaningful commentary for the adult facilitator. Simply purchasing and using a book such as this on a weekly basis with your grandchild is a foundational stepping-stone to deeper, life-long spiritual practices.

Kitchen table spirituality (hospitality and celebration)

> *Gracious inner space gives others room to play, question, and converse; room to be heard and understood; room to reveal themselves as they choose. Hospitality is essentially an expression of love. It is the act of sharing who we are as well as what we have.* —Marjorie Thompson, *Soul Feast*

As I wrote in my previous book, *Kingdom Family*, I am fascinated with the word *hospitality* and find it interesting—and rather dismaying—that this amazingly rich word has been reduced to be synonymous with entertaining. The root word from Latin is *hosp*, the same root as words such as *hospital*, *hostel*, or even *hospice*.

Hospitality does not mean throwing elaborate parties, although it might be a *reason* for throwing elaborate parties. It is a willingness to open your heart and home and life to others without trying to impress. At its root, hospitality is a means of service. True hospitality is a means of grace. As Marjorie Thompson wrote in the quote above, it is a "gracious inner space giving others room to play, question, and converse; room to be heard and understood; room to reveal themselves as they choose."

I recently read an end-of-the-year Instagram post from a friend who is a young mother. In a long reflection on family life, she wrote that in the past she felt ashamed of her home by comparing it to others; however, during the year just passed, her watchword had been #enough. She wrote that she had spent the past year intentionally allowing herself to love a home that had previously brought feelings of shame. "I snuggled my girls without wondering what I should be doing instead." The spiritual gift of hospitality is a realization of *#enough*.

The question you may want to consider is not how do you show hospitality to your grandchildren, but rather, in what ways do you invite your grandchildren into places of hospitality *with* you—into places of *enough*? As with the practice of service, compassion, and solidarity, the intentional practices of hospitality are a means of inviting your grandchildren into an alternative worldview and value than that so often modeled in the North American culture.

"There is a desperate need today for homes that can be open to one another. The old idea of the guest house has been made obsolete by the proliferation of modern motels and restaurants, but," writes Richard Foster, "we may seriously question whether the change is an advance" (Foster, 2002, 120). I wonder if you could invite your grandchild to help you plan for hosting out-of-town guests?

In our home, when our children were teens, we hosted a young Palestinian man for eleven months while he was studying for his Masters degree. There may have been inconveniences for us all, and some might say we ought to have paid for him to rent a room nearer the campus; however, the benefit in both his life as well as ours was a gift that paying money for convenience would never have given to him, to us, and especially to our teens who were observing and learning what the practice of hospitality might really feel like in their own home. Are there opportunities for you to open your home to missionaries on furlough or to persons from other cultures working on graduate degrees in your area? How might inviting and accommodating the practice of hospitality impact your grandchildren through the years?

The practice of hospitality might take the form of inviting your grandchildren to serve alongside you at a food pantry or soup kitchen or baking cookies for neighbors. It might also look like asking if they'd like to come and help prepare and clean up for a community gathering. When our children were younger and we lived far away from family, we decided to prepare, then pack up a Thanksgiving dinner, drive into Emmaus ministry headquarters on the north side of Chicago, where people from the streets gathered to celebrate the feast. I look forward in intentional hope that such opportunities will avail themselves when our grandchildren are older.

The act of hospitality with grandchildren holds the potential of bringing them further up and further into the practice of living life with deeper purpose. Perhaps a foretaste of becoming *real*?

Giving and receiving blessings

Being blessed with mutual blessing can release the original grace we were born with. That is the only risk involved. Who knows what will happen if gracefulness overwhelms the church? —Jerome Berryman, *The Spiritual Guidance of Children*

When my husband was born his paternal grandmother was on her death bed. She'd been waiting there, on that death bed, for awhile. No one was really sure why she kept hanging onto life. But then my husband, her first grandchild, was born and my in-laws brought their new tiny baby to visit his grandmother. When she saw him she rallied. Then with unimaginable strength in one so close to death, she took him in her arms, lifted him up, and pronounced a blessing on him. Within just a few day she died. It seemed to all the family that she'd simply been waiting to give her first grandson a blessing before she left.

Giving and receiving a blessing is an ancient practice. There are lots of examples in biblical history where folks gave and received blessings. Giving a blessing is a call for God's power. It is a type of prayer that says, *may it be so!* A blessing invites God to be present with us, in us and through us. A blessing is sometimes referred to as an *anointing*. (Think, for example, of when the prophet Samuel anointed the boy David.) When someone blesses you they are calling on God to give you a special purpose. A blessing means you and I can go beyond our limits to live a life unlimited because God is part of it.

A blessing is a very tangible way of practicing true hospitality, and I cannot think of a richer means of bringing your grandchildren into a space of reflection and belonging than by giving them blessings and also being willing to name and receive blessings from them. After all, how can we give something that we are not willing to receive? Praying for one another is, of course, valuable as well as commanded of us in Scripture; however, while a form of prayer, a blessing is a different mode of prayer.

INVITATIONS TO GO FURTHER UP AND FURTHER IN

My friend Marcia Stroup, a marriage and family therapist, whose grandparenting story of giving blessings is found in the bridge following this chapter, reminded me of a book titled *The Blessing*, written by Gary Smalley and John Trent. It recommends giving a specific blessing to those in your sphere of influence. God gave Abraham a special blessing that was to last for many generations to come. However, Abraham and Sarah had to wait patiently for many years for Isaac to pop onto the scene. As Marcia was sharing her story with me, she recalled Psalm 78:4, "We will tell the next generation the praiseworthy deeds of the Lord, his power, and the wonders he has done." It is in giving a blessing to others that we indeed walk in the ways of the Lord and the Lord blesses those in future generations even after we have passed into the next life. Why? Because the story and impact of blessings given and received, as well as the acts of praying into the lives of our children or grandchildren, has a powerful effect on their future.

As a marital/family therapist of many years, Marcia shared with me that she has seen the truth of generational blessings (but also curses) in those with whom she has worked. She shared with me that while working with psychology graduate students and clients, she coached them to hand back the injunctions or covert rules of past generations that had created dysfunction in their lives, rather than passing them on to their children. After all, she said, what is not passed back is passed on. Blessings—and also curses—have generational power over future generations.

I heard a story once about a father that regularly gave his children a blessing as they headed out the door to school or daily activities. He would put his right hand on their head and ask God to bless them by saying something like, "May you always know who you are and whose you are." The story goes that when his oldest daughter grew up, her parents helped to move her into her first college dorm. As they left her there in the dorm room and walked downstairs to their car in the parking lot, it felt like the end of an era as they left her there to begin a new life that they were less part of than ever before. Then they heard her calling from her dorm window, "Dad! Mom! You forgot to give me a blessing!" Of course! How could they have forgotten? They came back upstairs where Dad laid his hand on her head and pronounce a blessing for her character and for her future. Then when they left her and walked toward the car, they did so with lighter steps, knowing the assurance that God was with her, even when she was growing up and leaving home and beginning this new era in life.

While I was a children's pastor, I was responsible for giving a short message before the children left *big* church for Sunday school. Not wanting them to just walk out of congregational worship without a sense of belonging and understanding that this was their church at worship and that they were an important part of this congregation, I began inviting the children to stand in front of the congregation and raise their right hand to pronounce a blessing on the congregation by saying, "May the Lord be with you as you worship him." Then the congregation was invited to raise their right hands and pronounce a blessing on our church's children by saying, "And may the Lord be with you as you learn to follow him." Whenever we give a blessing we are reminded that we are participating in God's reality and inviting that reality into our lives.

The thing about blessings is that they are often easier to say and do than a prayer—they fit easily into our relationships, even with non-believers. Where asking a prayer may seem threatening, almost anybody will be willing to receive a blessing. Another thing about blessings is that they are almost always welcomed from grandparents. You can find a list of blessings, for all occasions, in the bridge following this chapter.

Yet another beautiful and visible way of giving a blessing is to revive the ancient faith tradition that has been practiced since the end of the Middle Ages and most often takes place during the church season of Epiphany or right after the new calendar year begins. The letters C, M, and B are usually traced on the doors of the home—usually the front door entrance; however, it could also be marked on an apartment, or dorm room, bedroom, or office door. C for *Christus*, M for *mansionem* and B for *benedicat*—all of which is Latin for "May Christ bless this dwelling." Paint might be used but most often the letters are traced with chalk or even with a finger dipped in oil or water. The three letters are then surrounded on either side by the century and the year and plus (+) marks are often added. For example: 20 + C + M + B + 20. Frederica Mathewes-Green, an Antiochian Orthodox, describes using newly blessed water in her church during Epiphany season (the blessed water represents the water of baptism). At some point between Epiphany (January 6) and the beginning of the season of Lent each year, every church home in her parish is visited by the priest and sprinkled with the water as a symbol of carrying the parishioners' baptism home (Gross, 2009, 85). After the water is sprinkled and prayers invoked, the inhabitants of the home may then be invited to take chalk and write the year and blessing on or above the door as a constant reminder and blessing to all who enter there.

INVITATIONS TO GO FURTHER UP AND FURTHER IN

All of these Christian practices, as well as many others, when done in community, and done visibly before our grandchildren, have the potential of taking both us and the grands into a deeper place of purpose and belonging, of taking us further up and further in. Perhaps this is a gift we may want to make an effort to give to our grandchildren.

Bridge 5: Stories of Redemption

Personal stories from ordinary grandparents on living your faith in creative and meaningful ways with grandchildren.

Camp Nona & Pop-Pops: Adventures & Memory-Making
. . . by Robbie Castleman

Using road trips for cultivating our relationships with our grandchildren has blessed us and them more than we anticipated when we began. From the time they were potty trained we have taken our grandchildren on a variety of road trips. Our grandkids have TOGs (The Other Grandparents) that lived near Orlando and Los Angeles—so trips to Disney and theme parks were already taken. We decided to focus on real places and nature adventures instead. We had T-shirts made for each of us with some sort of symbol for the general area or theme for each trip.

At first these road trips were five days to a week and started fairly close to the youngest child's home with day trips to branch out. So, when little Anna moved with her parents from Pennsylvania to Chicago, her older cousins went with us up to Chicago and we stayed in a downtown Chicago hotel and had a blast exploring her new hometown with her. We did this again the summer Anna and her family moved to a new home several years later. Tate's first *Camp Nona and Pop-Pops* was about ninety minutes from his home and we explored New Orleans!

As the kids grew our road trips grew to include Niagara Falls, Canada to the Grand Canyon, Mount Rushmore to Branson, Missouri. We stayed in hotels with family suites and started *CampLympics* with all sorts of races and challenges in the pool every night. Our grandkids had a blast, but an extra life lesson evolved as we always included other children who wanted to join in. Our kids learned early on how to cross bridges and introduce themselves to new people, to include others in our fun.

When the kids were in late elementary and junior high, we built our road trips around more specific themes. We took a road trip that included Civil War sites and talked about issues surrounding that conflict. We took an American history trip that wound its way from Memphis's Lorraine Motel, where Dr. King was assassinated, to Jamestown Virginia, to Mount Vernon to Washington, DC and the Ford Theater, the site of Lincoln's assassination. The subtitle of our T-shirts that year was, *The Good, the Bad and the Really Ugly.* All of us talked about race relations and the Christian faith throughout that trip. We'll never forget going to the Ford Theater the day after a young white man killed nine African American Christians in a South Carolina congregation. The African American ranger at the Ford Theater began his presentation by a stunning a capella rendition of the "Battle Hymn of the Republic (My Eyes Have Seen the Glory!)" with tears streaming down his face. We all spoke at some length to him after the program and shared his grief and his faith together.

A few things continue to surprise us about these road trips. One is the blessing it has been for our two sons and their precious wives to have time to be *just us* for six to ten days. Another surprise is really learning to recognize and appreciate the trust these parents have in letting us, year after year, shepherd their dearest treasures. To be trusted like this is a subtle but eloquent testimony to what our sons and daughters-in-love really think of us. What a blessing. Finally, two other road trip ideas that our grands have treasured. *The Nona Nevada Trip* in the summer of their sixth year. Nona (Robbie) was born and raised in Nevada but married into the deep south. So, just the six-year-old and Nona would take a trip *home* to see where she grew up—just forty-five minutes from Lake Tahoe. And during each child's ten-year-old summer, we took each one out of the country to a place (within reason) of their choosing. For the entire year before the trip (to Paris, to London, to Oslo . . . !) we sent the child information and history about the place we were going and this was the year they got a point-and-shoot camera for Christmas.

We'll finish crossing this bridge by mentioning, our commitment to these road trip experiences meant that birthday and Christmas gifts were very minimal. We saved up all year for *Camp Nona and Pop-pops!* We asked the four older kids (ages sixteen to twelve) recently what they wanted us to write for Trevecca's book. Each had a *private interview*, but all four kids mentioned two similar things as especially valuable. The first was the broad variety of places we've been and what they learned just by going there, seeing the place, experiencing its beauty, or sharing its impact. The second was best summed up as "Well, lots of families I know aren't all that close to their family at all. But, every summer, I get to have cousin-time and be with you!" All the camp kids mentioned just being together and seeing our lives close-up mattered to them. From prayer times and travel-Psalm reading, to discipline and correction, to flexibility with schedule and how we handled negative times (Rocky Mountain inn we had reserved was found abandoned and shuttered when we arrived! Sudden window blow-out in rental van!) with both faith and frustration helped them know us well. And we certainly learned how unique each of our grandchildren is and how to pray for them every day.

BRIDGE 5: STORIES OF REDEMPTION

Rituals of Blessing and Bonding ... *by Marcia Stroup*

My husband Dale and I adopted our two children, Tom and Kay, as babies. We were thrilled to have a family of four. When Kay was sixteen, she was suddenly and tragically taken from us in a car accident, leaving a huge hole in our hearts that even after many years still deeply hurts. Our son Tom was married for twenty years and his wife was unable to have children. Five years after the divorce that subsequently took place, Tom married again, this time a younger woman. I remember clearly when he came into Dale's office and said, "You two are going to be grandparents!" Steve was then age forty-nine and we were shocked and thrilled because we never dreamed we would have a grandchild at our ages. During Susie's pregnancy, we were concerned because she had previously had a miscarriage.

At that time we took a trip to the Grand Canyon, and stopped at Sedona, Arizona on our return. While there we visited the Chapel of the Holy Cross, which is a truly unique sight to behold as it is built between two towering rock formations rising 200 feet from the ground with a 90-foot cross as the centerpiece. The front of the church is floor-to-ceiling glass, with a striking view of the Sedona valley and red mountains. They announced a special 5 PM service, which we attended.

At the end of the service, it was suggested that if we had a special prayer request, we could carry a candle in a lovely red glass covering to the altar and say our prayer. I felt very emotional in seeking God's favor for a safe pregnancy for Susie and a successful delivery of the baby. As I placed the candle on the altar, God's Spirit reassured me of the importance of this special prayer for a special baby and her mother and father. I believe strongly in prayer and this was a significant blessing and meaningful opportunity where I felt God's presence.

I remember seeing the little hand held up in the ultrasound at Christmas. Now our granddaughter was becoming a reality. As we anticipated the time of her birth, we were ready to leave at any moment to drive to Salt Lake City, where they lived. On the way Tom called to say the baby's birth was hindered because she had turned, and a Caesarean Section was required. I remember crying, praying, and feeling joy that she was nearly here. We arrived two hours after her birth and loved being able to hold this miraculous new life—our granddaughter! How could it be—waiting all of these years like Hannah for son Samuel.

Our daughter-in-law Susie needed to take a nerve medication due to infection after an Achilles surgery reconstruction in which the damaged Sural Nerve was removed. That resulted in Chronic Regional Pain Syndrome (CRPS). Her doctor discussed the alternatives with her for her pregnancy and gave her the needed pain medication to treat excruciating nerve pain and prevent seizures. This resulted in Anna being in the Neonatal Intensive Care Unit (NICU) for several weeks to detox from the nerve medication.

As a therapist trained in Emotionally Focused Therapy for Couples, I know of the importance of *attachment theory* in treating couples and families. Back in 1940 John Bowlby in his research of orphans who died in an institution, searched for the reason. He found this answer: the most basic need of man from the cradle to the grave is for a safe emotional connection with others on this planet—parents when we're small, and partners when we're grown. To matter to another that you can count on, who will stand beside you in danger and doubt, is a first priority. In recent years, much ongoing research on attachment affects how we deal with emotions in creating safe attachments in couples. Additionally, to encourage bonding, now fathers or family members often are present at the baby's birth or hold the baby shortly after birth.

I learned the importance of soothing with a soft, loving voice while tenderly holding our granddaughter in the NICU. The early attachment in the hospital was a priority for Dale and me. Dale had few emotions about this birth until his granddaughter was placed in his arms shortly after our arrival. He instantly bonded with her and fell in love, which continues to this day.

One night I was holding her, with Susie in the room. I received a call from my prayer partner and she said, "Why don't you give her a blessing?" When I returned to the room, I asked permission from Susie to do this and she agreed. I put my hand over her little head and prayed aloud for this precious baby—her present and future, expressing to God my fervent desire to bless this life with his presence. When we opened our eyes, Susie said she felt something happening to her! This simple blessing was a profound moment to remember.

BRIDGE 5: STORIES OF REDEMPTION

A couple of years later Dale and I planned a vacation to the Grand Canyon with our family—including our little granddaughter. On the way home, we spent a day again in Sedona and visited the Chapel of the Holy Cross. My prayer from that night in the Chapel was miraculously answered and I was moved to tears of gratefulness. The five members of our family went to the altar, thanking and praising our God and Savior for this most precious gift of life he gave to us all!

This early bonding has led to our focusing a lot of our time and attention on our only grandchild. We often have a sleep-over on Saturday nights, with lots of playing out of doors, ice cream cones, and cuddling; we play the piano, sing Christian songs together, read her Bible stories/other stories, and kneel in prayer together at bedtime. We give her our full attention and love. She has brought an unspeakable joy into our lives that has changed us forever. She has become God's miracle and blessing to us!

A Compilation of Blessings for Use in All Life's Seasons

A Blessing from children to their church family (and blessing received)~

Said by the children facing the congregation in worship:
May the Word of God guide you as you worship him. (or *May the Lord be with you as you worship him.*)
The response from the congregation: *And may the Word of God be a light to your path as you learn to follow him.* (or *And may the Lord be with you as you learn to follow him.*)

A Blessing for Leaving (traditional Celtic Blessing)~

May the peace of the Lord Christ go with you,
    wherever God may send you.
May God guide you through the wilderness,
    protect you through the storm.

May God bring you home rejoicing at the wonders he has
    shown you.
May God bring you home rejoicing once again into our doors.

*(I use this blessing whenever grandchildren—and other
    visitors—depart)*

A Blessing for Character (traditional Scottish Blessing)~

If there is righteousness in the heart, there will be beauty
    in the character.
If there is beauty in the character, there will be harmony
    in the home.
If there is harmony in the home, there will be order in the nation.
If there is order in the nation, there will be peace in the world.
    So let it be.

A Blessing for Peace (traditional Swiss Blessing)~

May the Lord, might God, bless, preserve you and keep you,
give you peace, perfect peace, courage in every endeavor.
Lift up your eyes and see his face, and his grace forever.
May the Lord, might God, bless preserve you and keep you!

An Advent Blessing~

May the gladness of Christmas, which is HOPE,
and the spirit of Christmas, which is PEACE,
and the adoration of Christmas, which is JOY,
and the heart of Christmas, which is LOVE,
be ours now and tomorrow and forever. Amen.

BRIDGE 5: STORIES OF REDEMPTION

A Night-Time Blessing~

Now I am so tired, Dear Lord,
Help me to sleep, restore my energy,
cover my feelings and watch over
my mind, body, and soul as I rest in you tonight. Amen.

alternative for a grandchild:
Now (name) is so tired, Dear Lord,
Help (name) to sleep, restore his/her energy,
cover his/her feelings and watch over (name)
mind, body, and soul as (name) rests in you tonight. Amen

A Blessing when a grandchild is sick~

May God's gentle hand hold you.
May God's powerful spirit heal you.
May God's peace surround you and all who love you.
And may you rise again to run and play and imagine
and know how very much you are loved!

A Blessing when a grandchild is afraid~

*(For noise and silence and dark and things that go bump
in the night, from Psalm 91:14–16, The Message)*

If you'll hold on to me for dear life, says God,
    I'll get you out of any trouble.
I'll give you the best of care
    if you'll only get to know and trust me.
Call me and I'll answer, be at your side in bad times;
    I'll rescue you, then throw you a party.
I'll give you a long life,
    give you a long drink of salvation!

A Blessing for a New Bible~

By the light of God's Word may you see where you're going.
May God's Word be a lamp for your path.
May the Scripture stories of all who have walked by God's
    light inspire you.
May their ancient stories mark the trail of your journey.
And may you always know that you belong to God's great family
    and learn to make these Holy Words your own.

A Baptism Blessing~

May the blessing of Christ come to us in this child.
God's blessing is mercy and kindness and joy.
Blessing comes to home and to family.

Three Blessings for a First Day of School~

1. May your staples never jam,
   Your pencils always be sharp,
   Your ink flow smoothly,
   Your Post-Its always be sticky,
   Your Sharpies always be bright,
   Your glue never clog,
   And your Mr. Sketch markers
   Always be smelly.—anonymous blessing for the first day of school

2. You're off to great places.
   Today is your day.
   Your mountain is waiting.
   So get on your way.—Dr. Seuss

3. May the road rise up to meet you.
   May the wind always be at your back.
   May the sun shine warm on your face.
   The rains fall soft on your fields.
   And until we meet again,
   May God hold you
   In the palm of his hand.—Traditional Gaelic blessings

   (See chapter four bridge for prayer after a school shooting)

BRIDGE 5: STORIES OF REDEMPTION

A Graduation Blessing~

May the road ahead be paved with hope,
May your opportunities for financial success
    not outweigh the opportunities for mercy,
May you continue to learn and grow in the years ahead
    and may you become more the person
God designed you to be as the years unfold.
May you practice patience with yourself and with others.
May your adventures outweigh your sensibility.
May your security be found more in truth and honesty
    than in manipulation and power.
And may you grow in wisdom and favor with God
    and people all the days of your life.

A Wedding Blessing for when a Grandchild Marries~
From Dietrich Bonhoeffer's wedding sermon from prison

Marriage is more than your love for each other. It has a higher dignity and power, for it is God's holy ordinance, through which He wills to perpetuate the human race till the end of time.
In your love you see only your two selves in the world,
    but in marriage you are a link in the chain of the generations, which God causes to come and to pass away to His glory, and calls into His kingdom.
In your love you see only the heaven of your own happiness,
    but in marriage you are placed at a post of responsibility towards the world and mankind.
Your love is your own private possession,
    but marriage is more than something personal—it is a status, an office.
Just as it is the crown, and not merely the will to rule,
    that makes the king,
    so it is marriage, and not merely your love for each other,
    that joins you together in the sight of God and man.
As you first gave the ring to one another
    and have now received it a second time from the hand of the pastor, so love comes from you, but marriage from above, from God.

As high as God is above man, so high are the sanctity, the rights,
   and the promise of marriage above the sanctity, the rights,
   and the promise of love.
It is not your love that sustains the marriage,
   but from now on, the marriage that sustains your love.

Two Blessings for a new Grandchild~

1. We gather to bless this child.
   We wrap *(name)* about with blessing.
   Spirit of God, guard *(name)* with watchfulness,
      closely surrounding, held firmly with love.
   And from the threads of the life that we share,
      weave *(name)* a covering of thoughts, love and prayer
   that can grow as *(name)* grows
      and will always be there.—from *Celtic Daily Prayer, Book 2.*

   A blessing to welcome and bless a child whose arrival follows a time of trauma and loss of many kinds (such as infertility, miscarriage, illness or death of an older sibling, or disruption and uncertainty of economic hardship).

2. Child of calmer waters, you come after the storm.
   May your tongue be the olive branch in the dove's beak.
   May dry land always be granted: a firm place to set your foot;
      a clear but unfamiliar stride to take.—from *Celtic Daily Prayer, Book 2.*

A House Blessing~

May God bless this house from roof to floor,
   from wall to wall, from end to end,
   from its foundation and in its covering.
In the strong name of the triune God,
   all disturbance cease, captive spirits freed,
God's spirit alone swell within these walls.
We call upon the Sacred Three to save, shield,
   and surround this house, this home, this day, this night,
   and every night.

—from Claiborne, Wilson-Hartgrove, Okoro, *Common Prayer*

BRIDGE 5: STORIES OF REDEMPTION

A Kitchen Blessing~

May all who enter here
FEEL the warmth of belonging,
SMELL the goodness of bounty;
TASTE the richness of God's good gifts of food and drink;
HEAR the laughter and join in the conversations;
and KNOW this as a place of welcoming hospitality.
May all who leave this place
    carry in their hearts the hope of returning again
    and know that they will always be received as Christ. Amen.

A Compilation of spiritual practices and ways of praying with grandchildren

How do you pray with grandchildren and not make it feel pushed? Here are some ideas for adding the practice of prayer in your grandparenting/grandchild relationship.

Sitting still with eyes closed is a traditional way to come to prayer. Prayer can be very still and peaceful, but prayer can also be active by yourself or especially with children by many parts of our body and mind. Prayer can be touching, feeling, and exploring.

Below are four ideas for praying with children. These prayer styles aren't anything new. They are actually quite old, with long histories in the church.

Praying with Your Eyes

Praying together is a part of the Christian faith. But we are not always together. So over the years, common prayers have been written down in books so that we can be praying the same prayers at the same time of the day. In this way, even when we aren't together, we can pray together. Prayers from these books can be said any time of the day, but many Christians schedule these *common prayers* to be said in the morning as you wake, or in the evening as you go to sleep. There are some lovely new as well as old books of *Common Prayer* that are open to all Christians, not just certain churches or denominations. Three excellent examples for grandparents to share and pray from alongside grandchildren are:

- *Common Prayer for Children & Families.* Jenifer Gamber and Timothy J. S. Seamans. Illustrations by Perry Hodgkins Jones. Church Publishing Inc. 2020.

- *Common Prayer: A Liturgy for Ordinary Radicals.* Shane Claiborne, Jonathan Wilson-Hartgrove, and Enuma Okoro. Zondervan, 2010.

- *Celtic Daily Prayer, Books 1 & 2.* A collection of prayers, liturgies, and meditations taking readers deeper. Compiled by the Northumbria Community. HarperCollins. 2002 & 2015.

Examples of classic prayers from the Christian faith for the morning and evening:

- Morning prayer:

  Lord God, almighty and everlasting Father, you have brought me in safety to this new day. Preserve me with your mighty power, that I may not fall into sin, nor be overcome by adversity; and in all I do direct me to the fulfilling of your purpose; through Jesus Christ my Lord. Amen.

- Evening prayer:

  Watch, O Lord, with those who wake, or watch, or weep tonight and give your angels and saints charge over those who sleep. Tend to your sick ones, O Lord Christ. Rest your weary ones. Bless your dying ones. Soothe your suffering ones. Shield your joyous ones, and all for your love's sake. Amen.

Activity: Write your own prayers to share. With a grandchild or covenant group, write prayers of your own creation that are unique and timeless for your family and/or community. Perhaps you and your grandchild might find meaning in writing your own morning and evening prayers together, remembering that you both are praying them each day . . . even when apart.

BRIDGE 5: STORIES OF REDEMPTION

Morning prayer is a prayer of thanks and praise for the new day and for salvation in Jesus, symbolized by the rising sun.

Evening prayer is the Christian way of closing the day; a reflection on the good of the day and reconciliation for the wrongs done.

If you like, you can start collecting some of your shared prayers in a book and add to them over time. *This could become meaningful as the grandchild picture books from a story of a blessing by Susan Ballard in the bridge following chapter one in this book.* Maybe you could write a special prayer for birthdays and one for holidays.

Activity: Baptism Day Remembrance. I have found that sending a special handmade card with a written prayer and picture for remembrance of baptism days is a simple way to speak meaning into a holy remembrance.

Praying with Your Fingers

Activity 1: Create your own Prayer Beads (you don't need to be Catholic to use this simple prayer tool)

Traditional prayer beads are made up of twenty-eight beads divided into four groups of seven, called weeks. In the Judeo-Christian tradition, the number seven represents spiritual perfection and completion. Between each week is a single bead called a cruciform bead as the four beads form a cross. The invitatory bead, calling us to prayer, is between the cross and the wheel of beads. The total of beads is thirty-three, the number of years in Jesus' earthly life. The circular nature of the beads reminds us of the sense of completeness that one gains from a relationship with God.

How to make traditional prayer beads:

What You'll Need:

28 8mm beads (small beads)

4 12mm beads (cruciform beads)

1 white stone (invitatory bead)

1 cross pendant

1 32-inch piece of waxed linen cord

1. Fold the piece of linen cord about one third of the way down and thread the folded end—the end that is bent—through the eyelet of the cross. Place the loose ends through the loop and pull them tightly to secure the cross. Tie a small knot near the cross.

2. Thread both ends of the cord through the white stone invitatory bead and tie a small knot above it.

3. Thread one end of the cord through one cruciform bead, and the other end through the same bead in the opposite direction.

4. On the longer end of the cord, thread seven small beads, followed by one cruciform bead. Repeat this process twice more.

5. The pattern should be seven small—one cruciform—seven small—one cruciform—seven small—one cruciform—seven small.

6. Take this long beaded length of cord and thread it back through the first cruciform bead. Adjust the tension to your liking and tie a square knot with the two loose ends snugly under the first cruciform bead. Snip the ends of the cord.

A Sample Prayer to use with your prayer beads:

A Prayer for Children

Cross: *Hi God—I'm here and want to talk to you.*

Invitatory Bead: The Lord's Prayer

1st Cruciform Bead: *Thank you for everything*

1st Set of Weeks Beads: Specific things you are thanking God for (examples: mother, father, sister, brother, best friend, pet, snow, flowers, toys, answered prayers)

2nd Cruciform Bead: *Please help my family and friends*

2nd Set of Weeks Beads: Specific petitions for family and friends

3rd Cruciform Beads: *Please help me*

3rd Set of Weeks Beads: Specific personal petitions

4th Cruciform Bead: *I love you God*

4th Set of Weeks Beads: Specific things for which you praise God

—by Gabriele C. Whittier (may be reproduced without permission)

BRIDGE 5: STORIES OF REDEMPTION

Activity 2: Create your own nontraditional prayer beads

- Add one large bead (usually gold, white, or purple) to remind you to praise and adore God each time you pray).
- Add one small bead (silver, gray, or white) to remind you to pray for yourself.
- Next add a black bead to remind you to confess your shortcomings to God . . . and leave them there.
- Followed by blue bead to remind you to be silent before God and ready to listen.
- Add a wooden bead to remember that you are still a work in progress and pray for the character and faith qualities you are longing to develop.
- Next add beads for those you love and also those you have trouble loving so you are reminded to pray also for them.
- Add small blue beads to remember to pray for those who are sick, those who are lonely, and those who are depressed.
- Add a couple more beads for special concerns.
- Finally, add a large clear blue or green bead to remind you to pray for the world.
- But most of all, don't forget to just talk to God.

Praying with Your Imagination

Imagination is a wonderful gift God has given to humans created in God's image! We are invited to be imaginative and creative, we are invited to be storytellers who gather round and share wonder together. The whole of creation displays God's imagination, God's creative and recreative play! One of the most delightful ways to bring grandchildren into prayer is through their imagination and wondering.

Here are three meaningful ways to bring imagination into your relationship with children and God:

- *Imaginative Prayer: A Yearlong Guide for Your Child's Spiritual Formation.* Jared Patrick Boyd. 2017.
- *Spiritual Conversations with Children: Listening to God Together.* Lacy Finn Borgo. 2020.
- *Stories of God at Home: A Godly Play® Approach.* Jerome Berryman. 2018.

Actually, using this practice is easier than you would think. It simply means wondering out loud about the stories of God or any other story, or actually anything else you're talking about with children. For example:

- I wonder what Jesus thought when all the crowds showed up to listen to him talk about his father, God?
- I wonder what the disciples were thinking?
- I wonder what you enjoyed most about your day at school?
- I wonder if you made anybody sad? Happy?

Or questions such as:

- Do you ever wonder what would happen if you could suddenly fly through the air?
- What's the bravest thing you've ever done? The most challenging thing? Etc.
- What are two things you wonder about in life?

Reading with imagination is a little different. It is the close-your-eyes-and-imagine sort of listening to what God might be saying to you. Such as this small example from Boyd's book (listed above): *Imagine God's love for you is so great, and imagine God's love is like a light that is all around you so that you can feel it and see it and even smell it, because the love of God is also like a fragrant aroma* (Boyd, 2017).

And a small example from Borgo's book (listed above):

What is Holy Listening?

- A place where children receive undivided attention as they express themselves about the experiences of their lives.

- A "soul friend," someone who helps children recognize and respond to the presence of God in their lives.
- Confidential. We will never reveal what you say to anyone unless it is for his or her protection.
- Safe. Creating a safe space for grandchildren to be open and honest without any advice ... for the moment. (Borgo, 2020)

A grandparent can become a *holy listener* who helps the child recognize and respond to the movement of God in their experiences. *Holy listening* can look like playing with toys, expression through art, and talking with God using various means.

Praying with Your Feet

Activity 1: Walking the Labyrinth

- Using the labyrinth involves moving one's body while opening one's heart to prayer. All you have to do is follow the path and you will find the center. Unlike a maze, the labyrinth has no tricks in it. A typical labyrinth experience involves preparing oneself at the entrance and following the single path to the center, spending time in the center, following the same pathway out to the threshold, and then responding to the experience.
- On one's first walk in a labyrinth one may wonder if there is a right way or wrong way to do this. Pray on the labyrinth the way you like to pray in other places. Have a conversation with God about the things that matter most to you, offer words and gestures of praise, or present your prayer requests to Christ; there is no right way to pray the labyrinth! If you still aren't sure how to get started, simply repeat, "Thy will be done, Lord have mercy," or repeat the words of the Psalmist, "Be still and know that God is God" as you move through the labyrinth. Another simple way to pray the labyrinth is to pray for others on the way in, enjoy God's presence in the center, and pray for yourself as you move back towards the entrance ... which is also the exit.
- To draw or sculpture your own labyrinth: Look online! There are several patterns for drawing your own labyrinth on paper, making it of clay, or even creating a small labyrinth in your own backyard using

stones, rope, or sidewalk chalk. (This can become a fun and spiritual activity when grandchildren come to visit!)
- Create your own finger labyrinth: Finger labyrinths are small paper, clay, wooden, or even sand in a large flat round bowl that are simply too small to walk with your feet; perfect for "walking" with your finger!
- More ideas can be discovered on The Labyrinth Society website, www.labyrinthsociety.org

Activity 2: Walking with the Good Shepherd (an example from Borgo, 2020)
- Remove your shoes.
- Take three deep and slow breaths.
- Begin to walk slowly while praying the following.
- Close your eyes and imagine that you are a sheep and that God is the shepherd.
- Pray the following words as you walk (the labyrinth or the Prayer Trail)

> *God is my Shepherd and I am a sheep.*
> *God makes sure I have everything I need.*
> *God leads me to green pastures where I can lie down and rest.*
> *God leads me to green pastures where I can have sweet grass to eat.*
> *God shows me where there are pools of water so I can drink.*
> *God heals all the parts of me that are broken or hurt.*
> *Sometimes I walk through dark valleys, sometimes through a death valley.*
> *But I am not afraid because my Good Shepherd is with me.*
> *He walks next to me.*
> *His trusty shepherd's crook makes me feel safe.*
> *You, Good Shepherd, take care of me even when I am surrounded by enemies.*
> *You give me food, good food.*
> *You like me, choose me, when no one else does.*
> *Good is all around me.*
> *Mercy is all around me.*
> *You are my home, Good Shepherd, I live in you and you live in me.*
> *Forever.*

BRIDGE 5: STORIES OF REDEMPTION

- When you get to the center of the labyrinth, take three deep breaths. Talk with Jesus about how it feels to be a sheep. As you walk out of the labyrinth pray Psalm 23 again. As you near the end, thank Jesus for taking a walk with you in your imagination. Invite Jesus to keep talking with you. (Borgo, 2020)

Activity 3: Prayer Trails are another way to get out there and pray using your body. Many prayer trails are in a natural environment, and this tends to add to their appeal. It's nice to get away from all the noise and busyness of life. We get to move and be a part of the trail as the words of the trail become a part of us. Prayer trails also provide a space for us to listen. Many times we talk to God but we forget that God is also talking to us. The trail has space built into it which allows us to reflect on what we are reading, thinking, and experiencing. Perhaps the gift of following wilderness trails is the reason my husband and I love our nickname, "the camping grandparents," bestowed on us by our grands!

- *Idea for the prayer trail*: Decide on a prayer or perhaps a psalm and divide it up into phrases or sentences, just something long enough so that you have a thought to reflect upon. Use 3 x 5 note cards and markers and write each phrase of your prayer on a separate note card. Choose an area to become your prayer trail. This can be a trail through the wilderness, or simply a hallway, a fence outside, or even trees in your backyard. Take some tape for a fence or hallway or small stones for outside and attach your cards. You now have your own prayer trail. You can move together as a grandparent/grandchild pair or individually. Take time. Think about what the words say, and most importantly, listen for God! This can easily be set up when grands come to visit.
- The most important part of prayer is to remember that:
    - Prayer is talking to God.
    - Prayer is listening to God.
    - Prayer is taking time for God.

God just wants to hear from you. There are many ways that you can pray; the hardest part is just taking the time. So try to find a time or two each day that is just for you and God. These times don't have to be long, just try and focus. Pray alone or with a grandchild is a gift to each of you and a joy to God!

Guidelines for writing an effective ROL *(Rule of Life)*

- *Keep it Sacred:* The Rule creates space in your life for Holy Spirit-powered transformation. It is how you intend to seek *the pace of grace*, rather than determining what pace you can survive. The Rule is written to be consistent with Scripture, promote receiving from the Trinity, and assist you to live as holy in the world.

- *Keep it Simple:* The Rule needs to be simple, basic. The goal is ordering and orienting your life by a few key practices. The simplicity of the Rule means it can be applied anywhere in your life. (This is even more important for young people.)

- *Keep it Short:* The Rule should be short, especially for young people, or as you begin one for the first time. Clearly each idea or line of the Rule could be expanded to include more specifics, but take time to ensure that no element can be condensed or left out. The Rule should be something that you can readily remember.

- *Keep it Sincere:* The Rule is intended to be your genuine expression of a sincere desire to continue the godly life of a disciple. The Rule is meaningless if you don't mean it.

With a clearer understanding of a Rule of Life, it's time to get started. Grandchildren between the ages of twelve to twenty, with the guidance of leaders, parents, or grandparents, can create a Rule of Life by following these three steps.

Step 1: Pause and Pray. To begin crafting a Rule of Life, first pause and pray. (Pray on your own and, when it becomes comfortable, pray with your grandchild.) Challenge one another to set apart time and space, even as brief as fifteen minutes in a comfortable spot. Then pray explicitly for clarity, desire, and direction to craft a Rule with the guidance of the Holy Spirit.

- A prayer from Anselm of Canterbury: *Teach me to seek you, and as I seek you, show yourself to me; for I cannot seek you unless you show me how, and I will never find you unless you show yourself to me. Let me seek you by desiring you, and desire you by seeking you; let me find you by loving you and love you in finding you. Amen.*

BRIDGE 5: STORIES OF REDEMPTION

Step 2: Ask Questions . . . this can be a meaningful and even fun part with grands. Select a few questions from this list (but don't try to do all of them at once). When you have chosen two or three questions, take a moment to consider what each question is asking and then give a full and personal response. These questions are not in a specific order. Choose questions that feel comfortable discussing together between grandparents and grandchildren.

- What is the foundation of my life? What principles and ideals do I desire to drive me as a person?
- When and how often will I pray? Read the Scriptures?
- What activities of life will I consider to be essential?
- What specific activities will I or won't I engage in?
- What will my eating, exercising, and sleeping habits be?
- How will I find health in friendships, school, home, and work?
- What practices will I seek to engage in on a daily/weekly/monthly/yearly basis?
- Where will I engage in these disciplines? What time of day/week/month/year?
- What spiritual disciplines will I share with a spiritual friend(s) to join in together?
- What additional activities or practices are important, given my personality?
- How will I incorporate these into the rhythm of my spiritual practices?
- What practices are particularly needed because of negative patterns in my life?
- How will I need to adjust my schedule in order to consistently live this Rule of Life?
- Who will I trust to share this Rule with to hold me accountable to it, and to help improve it?

Step 3: Write and Live. Review your responses to the questions and begin writing your Rule. Remember, you are writing simple, short sentences that are actionable, reasonable, and measurable. Keep your

Rule in draft mode as you write and begin to live into it. Share it with a trusted grandparent, leader, or clergy person for both accountability and improvement on a regular basis. Make edits as you grow in holiness and as life changes. And live. *(courtesy of The Rev. Aaron Buttery, leader and facilitator for the NextGen Leadership team from Christ Church Plano.)*

A few books of spiritual practices for grandparents coming alongside grandchildren are:

- *Lectio Divina for Little Ones,* by Kimberly Fries. 2019. The book introduces children to sacred Scripture through the traditional practice of Lectio Divina. The practice follows four steps: Reading, Meditating, Praying, and Contemplating Scripture. This book explains each step and includes questions for the child to focus on throughout the process that are appropriate for their age. Children learn how to listen to the Bible, think about what it feels like to be in the passage, talk to God about the passage, and quiet themselves in the presence of God. For ages four to twelve.

- *Examination of Conscience for Little Ones,* by Kimberly Fries. 2019. This book leads children to recognize their sins and prepare for the sacrament of reconciliation. After calling upon the Holy Spirit's guidance, children are led through each of the ten commandments in order to recognize if he or she is following God's laws. Then, specific questions related to each commandment are posed at the child's level to ponder and take to prayer. For ages four and up.

- *Spiritual Conversations with Children: Listening to God Together.* Lacy Finn Borgo. 2020.

- *Stories of God at Home: A Godly Play® Approach.* Jerome Berryman. 2018.

- Godspacelight website. https://godspacelight.com/

6

Naming Sacred Spaces and Holy Time

Mustard seeds, kudzu and dandelions vs. mighty oaks, cedars of Lebanon and Redwoods. Being in a hurry. Getting to the next thing without fully entering the thing in front of me. I cannot think of a single advantage I've ever gained from being in a hurry. But a thousand broken and missed things, tens of thousands, lie in the wake of all the rushing . . . through all that haste I thought I was making up time. It turns out I was throwing it away.
—Mark Buchanan, The Rest of God

Holy, Holy, Holy

One of my earliest memories was being about three years old and standing on the pew between my mom and dad in the sanctuary of our Batesville, Mississippi Baptist church. I remember the exact row and location, just below the large stained-glass window picturing Jesus standing at the door and knocking, from Revelation 3:20.

Every Sunday we sat in that pew for morning worship. I spent my time systematically taking off my black patent leather shoes and lace-trimmed white socks to find my barefoot comfort spot. It was right about at that point that my mother would pull out my *quiet purse* she had made from the bottom of a plastic dish detergent bottle to which she attached a crocheted drawstring top. When opened and folded down it transformed into a baby bassinet complete with a crocheted baby doll with a plastic head. On one particular Sunday morning, while the congregation stood to sing the old hymn, "Holy, Holy, Holy," the bassinet and my baby doll slept while I stood on that pew between my parents and felt what I now understand to be a sense of reverence. It was a wonder and reverence of being with my church family as they all stood, faced forward, and sang harmoniously to this same God that my mom and dad prayed to and read me Bible stories about.

In my three-year-old brain I was putting the puzzle together and realizing that here was a time and space of holy otherness. That experience was a pivotal point of transformation in my faith journey.

By the time I became a mother myself and also answered the call to become a children's pastor, I had become passionate about reading and studying the impact of corporate worship on children as well as adults who worshiped with children present. I was discovering from my own experiences and the research that children and youth greatly benefit from being integrated into the church's corporate worship, while adults desperately need them there in their midst.

Over the past several decades the church has convinced parents (and grandparents) of two faulty claims: one, that the professionals can do a better job of forming their kids into super Christians than they can; and two, that each generation can worship best within their own age demographic. Though research shows the flaws in these messages, church educators have been hard-pressed to reverse this trend. There is much research and many explanations to point to as a way of understanding how and why this shift in church worship and faith education took place over the last half of the twentieth century; however, addressing that research and those explanations is not the purpose of this chapter nor this book. Instead, the point is that our grandchildren—yes, even as young as three years of age—are capable of awe and reverence if we allow them, invite them in, and create holy spaces where encounters with the holy otherness of God may be encountered. I encourage you not to fall into the trap that tells us that children can only learn when they are being entertained. Children have a great capacity for worship that, sadly, adults too often nurture out of them.

When children are allowed to encounter a holy God rather than a cartoon figure, they respond. When children are engaged with *wondering questions* such as "I wonder how you see God in this story?" or "I wonder if you are part of this story?" they might amaze you with their insights.

NAMING SACRED SPACES AND HOLY TIME

Slowing down, taking time, seeking reverence, naming holy spaces, and JOMO

> . . . .*in Christ, urgent means slow.*
> . . . .*in Christ, the most urgent necessitates a slow and steady reverence.*
> *Life is not an emergency. Life is eucharisteo.*
> —Ann Voskamp, *One Thousand Gifts*

Life is not an emergency. Over the years, this simple statement from writer and speaker Ann Voskamp has become a mantra in my life. In a culture that is always on demand, the intentional and thoughtful ability to slow down, take your time, seek reverence in the daily, and name spaces as holy becomes a subversive activity. So much of our lives revolve around rush and hurry and demands of our time and space. It is difficult for most of us, and especially for young parents these days, to resist this constant draw on their time and attention, even as they try to live fully in the moment with their children. Grandparents have an advantage here. We remember when life was not so demanding. Of course we all thought life was demanding in the '80s and '90s when we were raising our own children; however, the life of young families is lived on steroids today.

Our daughter has a good friend who is a young mother with three children. This friend made a conscious choice to resist the rush and hurry and although they both live in Ontario, unlike Ann Voskamp who has the added buffer of living on a hog farm in rural Ontario, this friend lives surrounded by the bustle of inner city living in Toronto. Christina Crook is one of my favorite examples of a person who intentionally steps outside the busyness of life and seeks JOMO (the title of her book, her TEDtalk, her podcast, and her website). JOMO is *The Joy of Missing Out: Finding Balance in a Wired World.* I often recommend her work to young parents as well as some grandparents. I know that Christina lives in the tension of finding balance while raising three children in the 2020s. Christina, our daughter, and several other young parents I know are seeking spaces of rest, reflection, and refocusing. I ask myself how I and others of my generation might come alongside them to encourage and support them and just let them know that we care.

Life is not an emergency. There is joy to be found in missing out. The psalmist of so long ago reminds me, life is more real and meaningful when I practice *being still and knowing that God is God*, and I am not.

Many grandparents may find themselves in a unique life stage with more discretionary time to live intentionally, even if not in a stage with discretionary money. Take heart if that is the case for you, because the ability to give the gift of time may be much more valuable to us and to our grandchildren than the ability to give the gifts that money can buy. Sometimes it is just a matter of stepping back and assessing the situation.

Even if not all grandparents feel the freedom of time, and even if your life might very well feel like an emergency, I encourage you to consider that in Christ, *life is eucharisteo. Eucharisteo* is an ancient Greek word meaning to express gratitude, to give thanks. It is used thirty-seven times throughout the New Testament. This ancient word envelops the Greek root word, *charis,* meaning grace, and the derivative *chara,* which is the Greek word for joy (VosKamp, 2011). Living your life within a perspective of eucharisteo allows you to see the joy and grace in all of life and communicate that with your grandchildren. Perhaps it is a matter of reimagining or re-envisioning life as a space for God's holiness to break in.

What might it look like for a grandparent to model life as *eucharisteo*, the gifts of grace and joy, or model JOMO (the joy of missing out) for children and grandchildren whose lives are often on overload? It might mean creating a physical space in your home where even young grandchildren learn to expect reverence. It may be the rituals surrounding a meal. It may be a quiet corner in your home or yard designed to invite your grandchildren to rest and reflect. Perhaps it is even in the music you have playing or perhaps through smells that trigger a sense of reverence. In his little book titled simply *Reverence*, philosopher Paul Woodruff writes that reverence "is an ancient virtue that survives among us in forgotten patterns of civility, in moments of inarticulate awe, and in the nostalgia for the lost ways of traditional cultures. We have the word 'reverence' in our language, but we scarcely know how to use it." (Woodruff, 2014, 1)

There are many possibilities for rekindling a sense of this lost virtue with our grandchildren. Reverence is a virtue, and by their very nature virtues grow in us through being used—through practice. Reverence develops when we make familiar habits out of our rituals and traditions. It can take place in our worshiping community when generations gather in named sacred space in awe of the majesty of a God who is treated not as our good friend who is there to bail us out, but rather a God who is named as holy. Both our practices of corporate faith rituals, as well as intentional rituals and traditions practiced in our homes, have the potential to invite us and our grandchildren into the experience of reverence (Okholm, in Larson and Keeley, eds., 2020).

In chapter three I shared the story about the time our oldest granddaughter woke me early to go in search of treasures in our little backyard. The simple act of searching for treasures and finding tiny flowers and hummingbirds bathing in the fountain created for us a moment of reverence. That day our backyard became a holy space because we sat quietly waiting for it.

Sometimes it is more a matter of learning to recognize and name our rituals and traditions. Anglican priest and young mother Tish Warren Harrison takes the everyday ordinary life of raising kids and shows how even the daily ritual of something as ordinary as brushing teeth can lead us to reflect together and recognize the rituals in daily life, as well as in our corporate rhythm of worship. In her book *Liturgy of the Ordinary: Sacred Practices in Everyday Life*, Harrison writes:

> We have everyday habits—formative practices—that constitute daily liturgies. By reaching for my smartphone every morning, I had developed a ritual that trained me toward a certain end: entertainment and stimulation via technology. Regardless of my professed worldview or particular Christian subculture, my unexamined daily habit was shaping me into a worshiper of glowing screens. Examining my daily liturgy as a liturgy—as something that both revealed and shaped what I love and worship—allowed me to realize that my daily practices were malforming me, making me less alive, less human, less able to give and receive love throughout my day. Changing this ritual allowed me to form a new repetitive and contemplative habit that pointed me toward a different way of being-in-the-world. (Harrison, 2016, 31)

Living in holy time and inhabiting the Story of God

Consumer culture always threatens to monopolize the feast days on which the church remembers saints like Nicholas, Valentine, and Patrick, turning those into little more than days to buy stuff in the name of cultural idols such as Santa, the Easter bunny, and green leprechauns. Too often we have forgotten the lives of the people for whom these days are named.
—Claiborne, Hartgrove, & Okoro, *Common Prayer*

Growing up and encountering worship in my Baptist church at a young age shaped the trajectory of my faith life; however, it was not until I became a Presbyterian that I began to learn about the rhythms and seasons of the church year. I don't blame this lack of liturgical instruction on the Baptist church because I know of several Baptist congregations that are very intentionally forming their worship around this ancient church calendar. I blame it more on the modernist culture that removed such practices from our church life. It was not until the dawn of what has been referred to as *postmodernity* that many Christians began to embrace ancient practices and liturgies. As Claiborne, Hartgrove, and Okoro write in the quote above, it is the surrounding *external* culture (see chapter four, internal and external cultures) that swoops in to shape us when we allow consumerist culture to show us how to celebrate.

Our daughter, son-in-law, and several of their friends are redeeming holy days from the culture and using them in ancient ways to shape their children, our grandchildren, in the Christian faith. For example, instead of waiting until December 25, they celebrate St. Nicholas feast day on December 6 by inviting their children to put their shoes out by the door for gifts to appear. Then they read stories of the historic St. Nicholas and talk about how his persona morphed into the Santa Claus we know today. Instead of piling on all the gifts and accompanying greed and stressors of opening every gift on Christmas Eve or Christmas morning, they at least try to spread out gift giving to fill the twelve days of Christmas that lead them up to the day of Epiphany, when they can celebrate Three Kings Day and maybe even get around to baking a *three king's cake* (recipes are easily found online and also in the bridge following this chapter). They learn about St. Valentine's and St. Patrick's real lives and create celebrations filled with meaning on those days, making them more than excuses to eat chocolate, buy flowers, or drink green beer. All of this happens with a little creativity and the help of some pretty amazing books or ideas for creating and living into holy time. (See the bridge following this chapter for a list of books, websites, and ideas to create meaning around seasons and holy days.)

Infusing our daily family life with a tool such as the historic church calendar invites us to realize in deeper ways what it means to be part of God's larger story that, like a golden thread, runs throughout the history of God's covenant people, reminding us that we belong to that story (see for example, the story of Abraham and Sarah as told in chapter one). As I say to the children when we put together the puzzle of the church calendar, *time* is like a golden thread. But what is time? I ask them. There is getting up time and going to bed time, there is school time and vacation time, dinner time and homework time and play time. Sometimes time moves too quickly, and we say we are running out of time, while other times seem to take forever and we feel bored, but, I ask again, what is time, really?

Then I begin to slowly pull the golden thread with my right hand out of my fisted left hand, saying, *some people believe that time has a beginning. At first time is new, but soon that new time becomes old time.* At that point I drop the thread with my right hand and then begin pulling it again from the left while saying, *sometimes people forget about the old time that is past and are only interested in the new time.* And I wonder aloud *if the new time feels more exciting.*

Finally, I come to the end of the golden thread and we wonder together if time has a beginning and an end, then I say, *I know what, let's tie the new time that is coming to the old time that has passed,* and I tie a little bow in the golden thread and time becomes a circle. Then I place the end that is a beginning and the beginning that is an end right before the beginning of the season of Advent, a time of getting ready to celebrate Christmas. Ah ha! *This must be why the church always tells time in a circle. The church is always remembering the past time and bringing it into the future time and each time we move around the circle of the church calendar every year we rehearse again the stories of faith, naming our faith family ancestors. Each time we begin again with the new year, we go further into the story of God while we also go further up into our understanding of our Christian faith.* Then while the children gather around I add the fifty-two small wooden puzzle pieces to the circle, just inside the golden thread circle of time.

We begin by adding the three great feast days of the church, beginning with Christmas when the church remembers the great mystery that God sent his only son into the world. I tell the children that *Christmas is so important that we have four whole weeks of preparation. Four weeks to get our hearts and our homes and our church ready to celebrate Christmas. We call this time Advent. Advent weeks are always purple or blue and when we see purple or blue in our church we know that we're getting ready for something very important.* After that I say, Here are six more purple puzzle pieces. I wonder where they go in the church calendar? *They go right before the great mystery of Easter when we remember that Christ died for the sins of the world, but we also remember that Christ didn't stay dead but rose again! This,* I remind them, *is a great mystery. The church adds six purple weeks just* to prepare our hearts, homes, and churches for the coming of the great feast of Easter! We call this the season of Lent. Following this I add that *Easter is so very important that the church has six more weeks of remembering, and these weeks are represented with white puzzle pieces.*

Finally, we arrive at the third great feast day of the church year. That is a red puzzle piece—the only red piece in the church year puzzle! And the children and I wonder together what the church always celebrates on this *red Sunday. The red piece is for Pentecost! That is the day that the church celebrates the gift of the Holy Spirit.* We add other pieces to the puzzle, a couple more white weeks for celebrating Trinity Sunday, which always comes right after Pentecost and is a time when the church recognizes the gifts of God the Father, God the Son, and God the Holy Spirit. Another white week comes at the very end of the old church year and right before we begin a new year in Advent (right beside the bow I tied in the golden thread); this is Christ the King Sunday. Finally we fill in the rest of the puzzle with green weeks for ordinary time—what we sometimes call the *green for growing* season—which fills in the weeks between Christmas and the beginning of Lent and the weeks in the season of Epiphany when we remember the light that is coming back into the world!

This is my favorite way of inviting my grandchildren and other children to find their place of belonging in the historic church's annual circle of remembering ourselves to God's ongoing, yet ancient, story.

Seeking after sacred time

> *I'm interested in the experience of sacred time, in our ability to feel the intersection of time and eternity at special places in the year . . . Sacred time is what makes the Church Year a genuinely transformative practice.* —Christopher Hill

---

Using a tool such as the church calendar as you are telling Bible stories to your grandchildren creates a visual of how the church orders time and also creates a visual of how we order time in our homes throughout the year. Jerome Berryman, the creator of the Godly Play® Approach to faith formation, recently wrote his book *Stories of God at Home*, in which he gives a lesson for parents or grandparents to use when telling the story of the church year calendar at home. In this telling of the story, children are invited to bring out family pictures to add around the circle of the church year to correspond to important family stories such as the day each family member was born. In this way our family story is integrated into God's story and the church's historic story. It is a beautiful and meaningful way to bring your grandchildren into a sense of belonging to something bigger than right here and right now. And it is surprisingly easy for grandparents to do at home, beginning as story time with young children.

Creating rituals and remembering ourselves to a story

Two of the greatest gifts Timothy's parents gave him and his siblings were a pair of rituals. Each morning, one of his parents would begin the day with a song, a prayer, and a reminder to receive and share Jesus's love. It was a simple ritual, but it gave each day a joyful sense of purpose and beauty. Similarly, just before turning out the lights each evening, they would take a few minutes to pray together, sing a short song, and reflect on where God was that day. No matter what good or bad events had taken place, Timothy would fall asleep with the faith that he, his family, and all the universe, were held in God's loving arms. —Jenifer Gamber and Timothy J. S. Seamans, Common Prayer for Children and Families

---

As James K. A. Smith explains, we are people who are formed in our rituals. Rituals, traditions, and habits form us into the people we are and the people we are becoming. Without named rituals and traditions we become people without a story. As we addressed in the introduction and chapter one, it was for this reason that children are occasionally driven to suicidal thoughts. Rituals, stories, and traditions create identity and belonging in our lives. Therefore, our stories, told through the actions of our family and faith-family rituals and traditions create a means for belonging that allows our grandchildren to develop into people of hope.

    I realize that some of the grandparents reading this book are not in their grandchildren's lives often enough to pass down rituals, traditions, or even tell family stories. This is a hard reality for many; however, that does not mean that we shouldn't name and practice our own rituals and traditions because in such intentional practices we become more grounded and reverent people for our own sake and the sake of those around us in life.

    My husband's cousin and wife have two beautiful grown daughters; however, when the girls were little the wife asked for a divorce and made it difficult for the father to be in the girls' lives, appearing to use them as leverage against their father. The hard part was for the widowed grandmother who suffered having these precious girls torn from her life. She continued to send Christmas gifts and birthday cards only to have them returned unopened by the mother. My advice to my aunt-in-law, which may also be helpful for your life situation, was to give it time and patience and save those unopened cards for the future when the girls are old enough to make contact on their own. There was no guarantee; however, shortly after the oldest got her driver's license she asked both her father and grandmother if she could come for a visit and today both girls stay in contact. Perhaps it was because the girls could remember the constancy of love and family traditions provided in their grandmother's home way back when they were very young that caused them to long to have that constancy of love in their lives again. It may also have been the traditions kept in the grandmother's home that reminded them of a safe place, a place of constancy, a place where they had roots and where they knew they belonged even as their mother moved from place to place and boyfriend to boyfriend. Also, it is valuable to point out that the grandmother never spoke badly of the mother's choices with the girls, not when they were young and also not today when they are grown.

Creating a space of calm in the chaos of daily life

Chaos and chaotic parents will rightly make children cry, withdraw, and rage—both inside and outside. —Richard Rohr, *Falling Upward*

Jenifer's parents required that, as a young child, she take some time each day to be by herself.
Their request annoyed her.
Jenifer wanted to play with her brother, talk with friends, or watch television.
But she would drag her feet to the hammock in the backyard, for her time alone.
Lying in the gentle rocking motion, staring up
into the canopy of leaves above, she felt her frustration
give way to calm as she noticed the warm rays of sun making their way through the leaves.
Their warmth opened her heart and she listened to a voice, its goodness and love.
Jenifer's parents wanted her to know herself and God.
—Gamber & Seamans, *Common Prayer for Children and Families*

The very act of naming rituals in our home as well as in our church creates an environment of calm against the rage of our current age. What if, like Jenifer's parents in the quote above, you as a grandparent could intentionally invite your grandchildren into a place of alone time? What might that look like in your situation? Perhaps a hammock in the backyard? Perhaps a drive in the car or a walk on the beach? Perhaps just the invitation of sitting in a worship corner when they come to visit? A place where they can light a candle and read a book and listen to calming music? There are so many ways that grandparents can invite grandchildren into such spaces and environments of calm. I encourage you to consider what that might look like in your family situation. For me, frankly, it is challenging since our grandchildren live in a different country; however, when we are together, I try to be intentional in creating spaces of calm that they can recognize as my gift to them. For us, hiking trails or walking long stretches of beach create such intentional spaces of calm amid life's chaos.

While creating spaces of calm we reach a place in our hearts, and especially in our grandchildren's hearts, that the surrounding culture seldom allows for. We live in this always on, always being entertained, always moving world. It is nice and also reorienting when we create spaces for calming the chaos. Sometimes we forget or even refuse to wait upon the Lord in our twenty-first-century culture in which we want everything, even holy things, to happen now and not later. Instead, as a model to our grandchildren and others, as well as for our own spiritual and emotional health, we may choose to live by *kairos* (holy time) rather than *chronos* (clock time). The rhythm of following the Christian year trains us to mark clear lines—or a clear circle—that trains us how to wait, and thus how to celebrate. The sharply drawn seasons of the church calendar serve to re-narrate the entire Christian story, enabling our lives to be renarrated and reoriented to the pace of *kairos* time, holy time.

The traditions that create family belonging

> *One generation commends your works to another;*
> *they tell of your mighty acts.* —Psalm 145:4

> *When we submit our lives to what we read in Scripture, we find that we are not being led to see God in our stories but our stories in God's. God is the larger context and plot in which our stories find themselves.* —Eugene Peterson

There are several places in the Bible, especially in the Old Testament, where the people of God are instructed to *tell of God's mighty acts.* Such instructions occur several times in the book of Deuteronomy. The best known is found in Deuteronomy 6:4–9 and is called the *Shema* (or *Shema Yisrael*, translated as *Hear, O Israel*). It is a Hebrew prayer that serves as a centerpiece of the morning and evening Jewish prayer services.

> Hear, O Israel: The Lord is our God, the Lord alone. You shall love the Lord your God with all your heart, and with all your soul, and with all your might. Keep these words that I am commanding you today in your heart. Recite them to your children and talk about them when you are at home and when you are away, when you lie down and when you rise. Bind them as a sign on your hand, fix them as an emblem on your forehead, and write them on the doorposts of your house and on your gates. (NRSV)

This prayer also serves as a reminder to us, as Christians, to love God with all our hearts, minds, and souls. And it especially reminds us as parents and as grandparents to *recite God's commands to our children and talk about them when we are at home and when we are away, when we lie down and when we rise.* It reminds us to *bind them as a sign on our hands, fix them as an emblem on our foreheads, and write them on the doorposts of our homes and our gates.* As mentioned in an earlier chapter, this is exactly what the friend of mine did when she invited her children to help her write prayers on the frames of their beds in permanent marker, so that as they laid down to sleep they were reminded that they were sleeping on their mother's prayers for them.

In addition to the Shema, the book of Psalms has some specific instructions such as the one at the top of this section from Psalm 145. Another is from Psalm 78, which I wrote about in chapter one of this book, where the psalmist reminds us of God's commands:

> . . . he commanded our fathers to teach to their children, 6 that the next generation might know them, the children yet unborn and arise and tell them to their children, 7 so that they should set their hope in God and not forget the works of God, but keep his commandments; 8 and that they should not be like their fathers, a stubborn and rebellious generation, a generation whose heart was not steadfast, whose spirit was not faithful to God. (NRSV)

We have no excuses to relegate the responsibilities of the biblical instruction of our children and grandchildren to others in the church, whether they be Sunday school teachers, youth ministers, or even pastors. This does not mean, of course, that we don't expect them to support us in the training of our children in the faith; however, it does mean that pastors and teachers and youth ministers should expect us to do our part in teaching the faith in our homes, whether that is praying with and for our children, telling Bible stories, or sharing our own faith testimonies with our children. Of course, all of us in God's church have the command to tell of his greatness to the next generation, and not just biologically related generations (I write more about that in the final chapter of this book). Therein exists the joy and responsibility of sharing God's story and our faith testimonies with *all* the children and youth in our church community, and this is especially good news for any of the grandparents who find themselves in that situation in which they are not invited or allowed to share faith with their own biological grandchildren. The church community is filled with children needing to hear from you and, who knows, like my husband's aunt, if you remain faithful, if you and I are willing to live at the pace of *kairos* time, holy time, the opportunity may arise with older grandchildren who seek you out and want to hear your stories and your testimony! Such things cannot be forced, but they can be invited.

Bridge 6: Stories of Sacred Space

We struggled to cling to God
. . . by Nancy (Nana) Pearson

As a mom and the children's ministries director at the church, I assumed that my children would always walk in ways of faith as they had through their growing up years. Each was active in children's and youth activities in our church, each went to camp and accepted Jesus as Savior. But at various points in their young adult lives, each made decisions to set their faith aside.

When our first grandchildren were born, our daughter enthusiastically brought them to Vacation Bible School, Kid's Klub Harvest Festival, and Family Advent Workshop at the church. We prayed with the kids when they spent time with us, but there wasn't a lot of faith practice going on in their homes.

Our daughter's diagnosis of cancer and her death in 2010 caused dramatic changes in the children's lives and in ours. In the midst of our grief, we struggled to cling to God and to try to make sense of her passing. The children struggled too; they were just eight years and eighteen months when their mom died. It suddenly became clear that these precious little ones that we loved so dearly would only be exposed to things of faith if we helped that to happen. So, we prayed with them at our house, we brought them to Sunday school when they stayed with us on the weekends, we enthusiastically participated with them in Vacation Bible School. And we prayed for them.

I know that God holds these precious ones (now nine and sixteen years old) in his hands and that he has plans for them that I cannot see. We continue to pray for their lives and their faith and their growth, even though we are not involved in their everyday lives. God has helped me to learn, as Nana, that the greatest gift I can give to my grandchildren is to lift them to him and allow him to hold them close.

Books and Ideas for Sabbath-Keeping and Holy Days Celebrations

A Recipe for Three Kings Day Cake:

On January 6, the Feast of the Three Kings—Trzech Króli (also known as the Epiphany and Twelfth Night)—a King Cake is served with a coin or almond baked inside. The one who gets it is king or queen for the day and will be lucky in the coming year. In the US, the lucky one must provide the King Cake for the next party or the next year.

Recipes vary by region. Some serve a French puff pastry-type cake with almond paste filling. Others favor a sponge cake with almond cream filling, and yet others enjoy a light fruitcake, as in this recipe.

Recipe makes 1 (10-inch) Bundt cake and 2 (6 x 4-inch) mini loaves of Ciasto Trzech Króli

Ingredients

Cake:

- 3/4 cup raisins (light)
- 3/4 cup dates (chopped)
- 1 1/3 cups walnuts (chopped)
- 1/2 cup dried fruit (apricots, chopped)
- 1/2 cup candied orange or lemon peel (chopped)
- 3/4 cup flour (all-purpose)
- 8 ounces/2 sticks butter (softened)
- 4 cups sugar (confectioners')
- 8 large eggs (room temperature)
- 4 cups flour (all-purpose)
- 4 teaspoons baking powder
- 2 teaspoons vanilla extract
- 1/2 cup brandy (or whiskey or orange juice)

Glaze:

- 1 cup sugar (confectioners')
- 3 tablespoons lemon juice (or orange juice)

1. Heat oven to 325 degrees. Lightly coat a 10-inch Bundt pan and two (6 x 4-inch) mini loaf pans (for gifting!) with cooking spray. Mix fruits and nuts and toss with 3/4 cup flour to keep ingredients from clumping together in cake batter.
2. In a large bowl or stand mixer, cream together butter and confectioners' sugar until light and fluffy. Add eggs one at a time, beating after each.
3. In a separate bowl, mix together 4 cups flour and baking powder and slowly add to the butter-sugar-egg mixture, combining thoroughly. Add vanilla and liquor or juice, mixing well. Stir in fruit-nut mixture by hand until thoroughly incorporated.

4. Pour batter into prepared pans. Insert a sterilized silver coin or almond randomly into the batter. Bake mini loaves 25 minutes to 35 minutes or more, and Bundt pan 45 minutes to 1 hour or more, or until toothpick tests clean.
5. Let cakes cool on a wire rack for 15 minutes before inverting onto rack to cool completely. Combine glaze ingredients and pour over cooled cakes, letting it run down the sides.
6. Make a paper crown, if desired, and place it atop the cake. Let guests serve themselves. Whoever gets the coin or almond is king or queen for the day and wears the crown.

Books for following the church year calendar with your grandchildren

- *Living the Christian Year: Time to Inhabit the Story of God*, by Bobby Gross. 2009.
- *Journey into the Heart of God: Living the Liturgical Year*, by Philip H. Pfatteicher. 2013.
- *The Christian Year: A Guide for Worship and Preaching*, by Robin Knowles Wallace. 2011.
- *Common Prayer: A Liturgy for Ordinary Radicals*, by Shane Claiborne, Jonathan Wilson-Hartgrove, and Enuma Okoro. 2010.
- *Celtic Daily Prayer, books I and II*, by The Northumbria Community Trust.

Books and websites to support Sabbath-Keeping activities with grandchildren

- *Keeping Sabbath with Young Children,* by Carol. S. Wilson. 2010. Sabbath is intentional time taken by individuals and faith communities to integrate the Divine with humanity and creation. Practicing Sabbath leads us to a fuller understanding of who we are as children of God. Young children (ages three to seven) lead us into new experiences of faith. These children are often most ready to practice the faith with us, and engage us in loving and caring ways. This book assumes that an adult will work with one child (or more) who probably has not yet developed reading skills. Practicing our faith is a lifelong process. When completed, this series will offer twenty-four practices in ten different life settings. This series can be used at any time or stage in your life.
- *Keeping Sabbath with Older Children,* Sharon Harding. 2010.
- https://beckyramsey.info/
- https://worshipingwithchildren.blogspot.com/
- https://www.worshipwithchildren.com/

7

Marking Trails for Those Who Come Behind Us

> *Where we fail to provide or give shape to meaningful and intentional rites of passage for our children, the surrounding market-driven culture will rush in with alternatives to fill the void.*
> —Steven Kang and Gary Parrett, *Teaching the Faith, Forming the Faithful*

God is in Montreal

I began this book with the ancient story of the *great family*. When our oldest grandchild was four years old, as I often do, I pulled my *desert box* out of the garage. It is just a flat Rubbermaid container filled with playground sand that I keep for telling my grandchildren stories from the Bible because so many of God's stories take place in the desert.

As we always do when our granddaughters visit (and even sometimes when other children visit), we placed the desert box in the middle of the kitchen floor, and with small wooden figures and smooth altar-building stones I told that story (paraphrased at the beginning of chapter one) of Abram and Sarai and God's *great* family. That may have seemed like the ending of that ancient biblical story from the book of Genesis; however, my story and my granddaughter's story continued.

Our son-in-law had recently left his ministry position as rector of a church in Montreal. It was the only place our oldest granddaughter could remember living in and the place where our youngest granddaughter was born. The week after their visit with us they would be moving to Toronto where our son-in-law would begin pastoring a new church.

At the end of telling the story of the *great family* I sat back and gave my usual invitation to wonder. *I wonder what it feels like to know that you belong to God's great family?* As Abram and Sarai wandered through the desert, they built altars as signs to others who travelled that way so those travelers would know that God was encountered in that place. I wondered aloud if people today build altars in *our* world to remind us that God is present and I wonder what those altars might look like? I wonder how many places God really is? At that point, in a small voice, my four-year-old granddaughter said, "God is in Montreal." My mind engaged and I quickly responded, "Yes, and I wonder if God is also in Toronto? I wonder if you can find any altars there to remind you that God is in that place?"

A few weeks after their move my daughter texted me to ask what story I'd been telling her, because as they were walking along the shore of Lake Ontario, our granddaughter stopped and pointed at the piles of stones in a fire ring on the shore and exclaimed, "Mama, look! God is here!" Even her four-year-old brain remembered and recognized the continuation of the story.

Where do you see God in your world? How about your grandchildren? When and where are they encountering signs of the living God in their world? What might you be able to do or say that will begin to build altars for your grandchildren to find and experience so that they will know that God is present in their world?

In the Old Testament book of Joshua, after crossing through the Jordan River, the Lord instructed Joshua to select twelve people, one from each of the twelve tribes of Israel, and instruct them to each choose a smooth stone from the middle of the river, carry them to the other side, and place them in an altar so that they would not forget God's faithfulness. And, in verses 6 and 7: "When your children ask in time to come, *what do these stones mean*, then you shall tell them that the waters of the Jordan were cut off in front of the ark of the covenant of the LORD. When it crossed over the Jordan, the waters of the Jordan were cut off. So these stones shall be to the Israelites a memorial forever." Building and also finding altars in your world with your grandchildren keeps us connected and hopefully faithful.

However, lest we feel angst and place a burden on ourselves for the responsibility of pointing our grands toward God, it is important to stop right here and be reminded of this famous prayer composed by Bishop Ken Untener of Saginaw, drafted for a homily by Cardinal John Dearden in November, 1979, to honor the martyred Salvadoran bishop Oscar Romero.

MARKING TRAILS FOR THOSE WHO COME BEHIND US

> It helps, now and then, to step back and take the long view. The Kingdom is not only beyond our efforts: it is beyond our vision. We accomplish in our lifetime only a tiny fraction of the magnificent enterprise that is the Lord's work. Nothing we do is complete, which is another way of saying that the Kingdom always lies beyond us. No sermon says all that should be said. No prayer fully expresses our faith. No confession brings perfection. No pastoral visit brings wholeness. No program accomplishes the Church's mission. No set of goals and objectives includes everything. That is what we are about. We plant the seeds that one day will grow. We water seeds already planted knowing they hold future promise. We lay foundations that will need further development. We provide yeast that affects far beyond our capabilities. We cannot do everything and there is a sense of liberation in realizing that. This enables us to do something, and to do it very, very well. It may be incomplete, but it is a beginning, a step along the way, an opportunity for the Lord's grace to enter and do the rest. We may never see the end results, but that is the difference between the Master Builder and the worker. We are workers, not master builders; ministers, not messiahs. We are prophets of a future that is not our own.

A future that is not our own gives us as grandparents permission not to feel guilty that we cannot do and say everything our grandchildren need to make it through this world and make it beyond this world into the full reality of heaven; however, it also gives permission to build a few altars in the world that grandchildren can hopefully point to someday and exclaim, "Look! God is here!"

Getting lost and finding yourself

> *Sometimes heroism is nothing more than patience,*
> *curiosity, and a refusal to panic.*
> —Leif Enger, *Peace Like a River*

While writing my first book, *Kingdom Family: Re-Envisioning God's Plan for Marriage and Family*, I had the unique opportunity to take a three-month sabbatical from my position as children and family pastor at St. Andrew's Presbyterian Church. I also had the opportunity to spend that three-month sabbatical living in a cabin on Bass Lake just outside Yosemite National Park while my husband was teaching for Azusa Pacific University's High Sierra program, a semester-long great books experience for students and professors living together in community and exploring the wilderness areas. While my husband and students were in class or off trekking the wilderness, I committed myself to spend my days writing in our somewhat rustic cabin by the lake. However, before I dug into my writing each morning, I also committed to two additional activities. One was reading and rereading several favorite books on spirituality; the other was exploring the relative wilderness in walking distance around Bass Lake. I explored along the lake shore and also took detours onto trails that led me up the mountains, beside streams, and to the discovery of several small waterfalls. My explorations took me over the dam or along the water flumes that carried spring snowmelt into the reservoir. Occasionally I felt lost until the trail led me back to the road. I never ventured far enough to get truly lost. During this time, I reread Annie Dillard's *Pilgrim at Tinker Creek,* about her experience of living alone in a cabin for a season. I also read Barbara Brown Taylor's *An Altar in the World.* Even typing the names of these books on this page bring a nostalgia for my time spent exploring the Bass Lake area.

One of my and my husband's favorite pastimes is camping and hiking and occasionally backpacking into the wilderness. We have enjoyed the moniker of the *camping grandparents* given to us by our grandchildren; therefore, one of our great delights is taking our grandchildren camping and hiking with us—and occasionally even getting lost—as together we experience nature through their eyes. There is something terrifying yet exhilarating about almost getting lost in the wilderness. Actually, once my granddaughters and I got lost for real in the wilds of High Park in the middle of the city of Toronto and had to call their father to come and find us! It is such experiences that not only create shared stories but also create a companionship between those of us on the trail.

In her chapter on "The Practice of Getting Lost," Taylor explains that "I have found things while I was lost that I might never have discovered if I had stayed on the path . . . I have decided to stop fighting the prospect of getting lost and engage it as a spiritual practice instead. The Bible is a great help to me in this practice since it reminds me that God does some of God's best work with people who are truly, seriously lost" (Taylor, 2009, 73).

This reminds me of that favorite Bible story of Abraham and Sarah. The thing is that Abraham and Sarah were willing to get lost. They were willing to take God at God's word and step out in trust without a map or a plan. I don't necessarily recommend that; however, Abraham and Sarah did it over and over again in the desert and it was in the very act of getting lost that they were in a position to encounter the living God. It was in the act of getting lost that their faith muscles were strengthened. We don't often get lost these days unless we are willing to leave the map and GPS behind and simply take time to wander. Getting lost with grandchildren can be a rewarding, albeit scary, experience; however, I highly recommend it. Where might you and your grandchildren get lost for a while? If you're not willing or physically able to brave the wilderness trail, I suggest that a good starting point might simply be a walk around the neighborhood while keeping an eye out for serendipitous encounters. This can be unexpectedly interesting, especially these day when nearly everywhere we go is by automobile.

Marking trails and looking for altars

As far back as I can remember I have been drawn to rocks and stacks of rocks. I am not sure why I have this fascination. Perhaps it is permanence, that they have been part of the earth forever and will be here long after I am dead. When I first discovered rock cairns stacked along trails, I was smitten. Here were stacks of rocks that served a purpose in not only announcing the trail, but also giving glimpses of those who came before me on the trail, fellow hikers who had the presence of mind to make my sojourn easier by putting out signs to direct my path. Rock cairns are also called milestones or mile markers, and in ancient Hebrew such stacked stones were called *ebenezers*, stones of remembrance. I like this unique word because in a time when some churches are trying to change every ancient word to familiar modern ones so as not to threaten the uninitiated or appear out of touch, the word *ebenezer* has stood firm. The 1757 hymn by Robert Robinson, "Come Thou Fount of Every Blessing" carries the verse, "Here I raise my ebenezer, hither by thy grace I've come, and I hope by thy good pleasure safely to arrive at home." This hymn and its mention of raising an *ebenezer* has become a mainstay even in praise worship, made popular again in 1994 by Fernando Ortega and later by others such as Chris Rice, Chris Tomlin, and the David Crowder Band. But to the point, such milestone markers have been used down through the centuries and are still used on trails today to announce a fork in the path, keep unsure travelers going in the right direction, and mark a sure way forward. This is what we desire to do as grandparents, point our children and grandchildren to the right path by leaving mile markers along life's journey to mark their way forward. What do these milestones look like?

As a children's pastor for a quarter century I helped develop what we called a *Milestones Ministry*, where children and significant adult(s) would participate in special age-specific events. Sometimes such Milestone events were only one Sunday after worship or one weekday evening; however, some lasted several weeks. Each Milestone opportunity was offered only once a year per age group and *always* included the parents and/or grandparents or other significant adults. The age-specific events included second graders going on a worship treasure hunt to learn about The Who, What, When, Where, and Why of our church's worship; or third graders receiving and learning how to find their way around a Bible; or fourth graders and their significant adult(s) learning about the sacraments observed in our church. The key to the Milestone ministry was making sure the parents and/or grandparents participated and learned alongside their children. This created an opportunity for the children to look to these significant adults in their lives as role models of faith. Why does this matter so much?

It matters, first, because we live in a culture in which our children and youth too often look primarily to paid children and youth staff to train them in faith instead of looking to those significant adults in their lives, and second, we live in a culture in which our children and youth encounter few named and celebrated milestones or rites of passage in our faith communities. As Kang and Parrett point out in their book, *Teaching the Faith, Forming the Faithful*,

> We in North America have been shaped by the powerful social rituals surrounding a young girl turning "sweet sixteen," [getting one's first driver's license], the prom for high-schoolers, engagements to be married, the multibillion-dollar wedding industry, the multibillion-dollar baby industry, and on and on. The need for meaningful rites of passage is inherent in our humanity, and the church is wise to address it. (Kang and Parrett, 2009, 331)

Old Testament scholar Bruce Waltke argues that "the opposite of remembering is not forgetting, but *dis*membering. In the broad culture of our day, as well as in much contemporary church practice, we have been effectively dismembering our children by stripping them of the memories [rituals and rites of passage] they so desperately need" (Waltke, 2002, audiocassette). Grandparents who take their role seriously may very well be in a prime position for giving name to those rituals our grandchildren desperately need in their lives so as to be about *re*membering potentially *dis*membered generations. As grandparents, we may be in positions to choose and name rituals and rites of passage for our grandchildren and fill those with meaning.

What are those pivotal times when you, as a grandparent, might encourage or bring about such recognized and celebrated milestones? We are pretty good at remembering birthdays or first days of school, but how about remembering and marking *faith birthdays*, aka baptism day? Or what about celebrating first Bibles and looking for ways to mark and infuse this rite of passage with meaning? What about noticing and celebrating when a grandchild moves from nursery to Sunday school, or from elementary school to youth ministry? Perhaps celebrating a first communion? How might grandparents play a role in bringing a faith component into high school graduation? Perhaps it might happen by encouraging your church community to mark an intentional ritual of moving youth from their strong youth group connection to their place of belonging and participation as an adult member of the church community. Such rituals around moving from youth to adulthood in church community can be important before they head off to college and the beginning of a new era in life; rituals of celebrated milestones in life create a sense of belonging that will equip them to make most life transitions well. At First Presbyterian Church of Glen Ellyn (Illinois), where I served as children's pastor, we had a group of mostly moms who came together each month to create care packages and handwrite love notes to send off to our church's college students, not only to show support and keep them connected, but also to give them a deeper sense of belonging within this church family by reminding them that they were loved and prayed for. This might be a beautiful role for grandparents to play in the church community, even or especially with our non-biological grandchildren.

There are so many faith markers in our lives that often go relatively unnoticed. For example, I keep our granddaughters' baptism dates marked on my calendar each year and send a card, usually homemade because such cards are not readily available from Hallmark. I add pictures of their baptism and Scripture verses and prayers and reminders that they belong to God's covenant people, that they are children of God. I am thankful that our grandchildren's parents remember to bring out and light each grandchild's baptism candle at the dinner table on that day, even though

I suspect it is occasionally because they are reminded when my card arrives in the mail! When you think about it, marking trails in life's faith journey is rather simple and yet carries such great potential for orienting our grandchildren's worldview.

I remember your honest and true faith

> *I remember your tears. I long to see you so that I can be filled with joy. I remember your honest and true faith. It was alive first in your grandmother Lois and in your mother Eunice. And I am certain that it is now alive in you also.* —2 Timothy 1:4–5 (NIRV)

A most valuable privilege of grandparenting is passing on the faith. Often this is an easier, more natural role for grandparents than for parents. I didn't realize this when I was a young parent and felt much of the burden myself. Although my in-laws were Christian and wonderful grandparents to our kids, they were not often intentional in the ways they sought to pass on faith to their grandchildren. As for my own mother, she was very ill most of their lives before dying when they were still young, and my father died long before they were born; so now it is my privilege to charge a new generation of grandparents—my generation of grandparents—to reflect on such a privilege that may be ours today. Especially when we consider the statistics written about in chapter four on becoming R.E.&A.L. with our grandchildren.

Bridge 7: Stories of Paying Attention

*Personal stories from ordinary grandchildren
on Marking Trails for Those Who Come Behind Us*

Modeling a Posture of Time and Presence for her Grandchildren . . . by *Jennifer M. Buck*

Before I was born, my paternal grandparents had taken a trip to Europe and during the vacation my grandmother had caught an infection that attacked her heart. She would end up needing a heart transplant, but for a variety of reasons she did not qualify, and as a result the doctors gave her six months to live. She defied that prediction and ended up living another twenty-plus years; however, because of the heart infection, she was bedridden and on oxygen.

My family lived in Orange County and my grandparents lived in Pasadena, so my childhood was often filled with Saturday day trips up to visit my grandparents, taking my grandpa out to lunch and catching up with my grandma by her bedside until her energy was spent and she needed to rest. My high school graduation is one of my few memories of her ever working up the stamina to leave the house. Her body was frail but her spirit was always full and her mind stayed sharp her entire life.

My grandma Virginia had been a librarian at the University of Southern California. Books were such a significant part of her life. One of the beautiful ways my grandpa cared for her was making weekly trips to the Pasadena public library to pick up her list of reserve books. As the world became more and more digital, my grandma enjoyed reading all that the internet had to teach and curating emails to all her children and grandchildren of articles about their interests and hobbies, various things she had learned, and so forth. Learning and reading became vital ways she stayed connected to her family even when there was geographic distance between us and her physical capacity was limited.

For me in particular, when I decided on a graduate school, I was thrilled that one advantage of attending Fuller Theological Seminary in Pasadena meant that I could spend more time with my grandparents. I was a commuter student trying to figure out what my schedule would look like; wanting it to include my grandma, I proposed to her that we have weekly lunches at her house. She loved the idea and took it one step further. She wanted to learn alongside me, as she was developing a Christian faith in the Lutheran tradition later in life (a convert to Christianity in adulthood through, alongside other things, the faith of my own parents). She was eager to read more theological texts assigned for my Masters of Divinity courses, so she suggested I give her my syllabi at the beginning of every quarter. She would get the books herself, and when we would have our weekly lunches, she would have done my weekly readings alongside me and we could have a salon-like discussion about the texts.

This generous idea turned into one of the sweetest memories of my graduate school years. I would often leave Fuller Seminary, pick up some quick lunch for us from Trader Joe's (my grandparents' favorite), and come to their house in Kinneloa Canyon for our time together. My grandpa told me she would often schedule her hair appointment for the day before because our lunch was one of her big activities of the week.

We would sit in her living room and she would bring out all her copious notes on each of the books, complete with observations and questions from her own background, rich with life experience but limited in theological training. I grew tremendously by learning how to better explain what I was studying, and her observations highlighted aspects of the texts that I might never have noticed. This would typically only last about an hour, but the conversations were so rich I would often leave chewing on ideas she said for weeks at a time. Before I even had language for it myself, she was encouraging me to critique the works I was reading from a gendered lens, appreciate the spiritual practices of early church mothers and fathers, and embrace the value of a more high-church liturgical perspective.

I started my studies at Fuller Seminary in 2007 and my grandmother passed in 2009, shortly after my grandfather passed as well. Those almost two years where we practiced this habit of reading the books together modeled for me a grandparent eager to continue learning alongside me (and from me!) as I learned from her, and more significantly, modeled a posture of time, presence, and engagement in the passions of her grandchildren. I knew how proud of me she would have been when I graduated with my Masters in Divinity degree in 2010. My parents hosted a small graduation party for me at one of my grandparents' beloved Pasadena restaurants, Burger Continental, and that felt like a way to honor them on that day.

When I finished my PhD and got my dissertation published, I dedicated my book to her, because I could see how much those few years really encouraged me in my academic journey and shaped my own theological thinking. I cannot think of a better way that she could have been present with me in that season as a grandparent than through our theological lunches and I carry them with gratitude into my own season of new parenthood.

The Gift of Multigenerational Community
. . . by Emma O'Brien

If you go to almost any modern-day evangelical Christian church today, there will be a lot of talk around the word *community*. There may be many different programs, groups, events, and opportunities to connect. However, true community cannot exist apart from intentionally built relationships.

Relationships that are formed not simply because you attend the same church, or the same small group but because you both choose to *see* one another. Both parties actively choose to pursue one another, learn from one another, and give and receive from one another.

Several years ago, this was the kind of community I was so incredibly blessed to be part of at Holy Trinity Church. I started attending the church primarily out of convenience—I didn't have a car, and the church met on my college campus. A few of my college friends joined me too. One of the first things that stood out to us as young college students were the age demographics. It was probably safe to say that out of the 100 people in the church service, we were the only few that didn't fall in the age range around forty-five to sixty. We honestly found this refreshing, though. After being around millennials all day, every day, it was refreshing to be around older folks. And we weren't the only ones who were excited about this. Many of the older church members made it a point to connect with us after the service. Sometimes we would talk for at least an hour on the outside patio. I was so excited to learn from my brothers and sisters in Christ who had been walking with God for so much longer than I had, and who had just lived through so much more of life than I had.

Then one day, I can't remember exactly how it happened, but we were given the opportunity to start Friday night dinners. A few different older couples in the church had decided to open their homes to us every Friday of the month, feed us dinner, and just wanted to get to know the college students in their church. We were all so excited. These Fridays quickly became the highlight of my week.

Growing up not having known my grandparents, these evening dinners and time spent together were especially meaningful for me. I can honestly say that since experiencing this deep level of intentional community at Holy Trinity, I have yet to find another church community that made the time and had the desire to cultivate such a deep level of relationship. I believe that much of what made these experiences so meaningful is that the relationships were multigenerational.

To this day, I still keep in contact with some of the couples that hosted my friends and me on those Fridays. One woman in particular has become a very close friend and mentor. I can't find the words to fully express how valuable and fulfilling this experience was, not just for my friends and me, but for the couples with whom we developed relationships. These experiences gave me a taste of true community, developed my spiritual formation, and helped me to form lasting relationships across generations. I would highly encourage every church, every community, to do something like this. Our world needs this more than ever!

Prayers for an Attentive Life

A Prayer for Being Present~

Lord, what will I pay attention to today?
Will it be those things that demand my attention?
The have-to-dos . . . The won't-waits . . .
The things that keep me too busy to see the important things
    in my life?
O Lord, grant me space to seek the gift of time well spent
Time to dwell in the eternal.
Time to discover the gift of joy in little things too often
    left undone.
Time to explore in the gift of peace even in the midst of
    my chaotic life.
Time to grasp the gift of hope for future generations.
And time to consider how I might make a difference in
    the lives of my grandchildren.
Time to pray.
Time to be a blessing.
Time to discern your presence in all of life.

A Prayer for Paying Attention~

Heavenly Father, I pray for the grandchildren who are not
    my own, not my flesh and bone.
I pray for young people who need older women or men
    to come alongside them on the journey.
Open my eyes, O Lord, to see those whom I might befriend.
Open my ears, O Lord, to hear their stories.
Open my hands, O Lord, to share myself with others.
Open my home, O Lord, to invite them in to sit around my table.
Open my heart, O Lord, to love all your children . . . that I might
    become a mentor and a friend.

A Prayer for the Blessing of Family~

(from Canadian Book of Common Prayer, 1962 edition, p. 732)

Merciful Savior, who loved Martha and Mary and Lazarus,
    hallowing their home with thy sacred presence.
Bless, we beseech thee, our home, that thy love may rest upon us,
    and that thy presence may be with us.
May we all grow in grace and in the knowledge of thee,
    our Lord and Savior.
Teach us to love one another as you have commanded.
Help us to bear one another's burdens and so fulfill your law,
O blessed Jesus, who with the Father and the Holy Spirit lives
    and reigns,
One God, for evermore. Amen.

8

The Grandparenting Effect on Non-Biological Grandchildren in Our Lives

Christian teaching has much to say concerning the choices we make about including persons in our families and continuing to be family for one another when the going gets rough. These are issues of Christian discipleship. —Diana Garland, Family Ministry

Even childless families often carry responsibility for generational care.
—Diana Garland

The best way to be formed in Christ is to sit among the elders, listen to their stories, break bread with them, and drink from the same cup, observing how these earlier generations of saints ran the race, fought the fight, and survived in grace.
–James Frazier, Across the Generations

Jesus was a teacher who kept folding in those outside of what was considered socially acceptable in his day, challenging his followers to think beyond their usual categories of inclusion. —Diana Garland, Family Ministry

Thinking outside our cultural box: the practice of learning to see differently

A couple of times in chapter one I used the term *grandchildren-in-faith*. This concept also showed up several more times in the reading of this book.

On the first day of class in my Family Development and Ministry course I ask a couple of questions: *Who in your life do you relate to as family?*; *Who belongs in your family?*; and, *Who functions as family to you?* For each of us, we have certain people with whom we are connected through our DNA; these folks can be defined as our *structural* family and, like it or not, we are forever linked to them even if they have no meaningful interactions in our lives. Yet, we all have other people that come into our lives and become our go-to people. These are the folks we would call in a crisis, the folks with whom we spend time and from whom we draw energy and comfort. This group of people in our lives are not exactly family . . . or are they? In her book *Family Ministry: A Comprehensive Guide,* Diana Garland defines this group as our *functional* family.

The concept of categorizing certain people as special in our lives potentially holds more meaning for us if we begin to categorize them as family, perhaps identifying them as *functional family*. The beauty and blessing lies in the fact that often those people in our *structural family* are the ones who also *function* as family to us!

These categories of distinction create a space for us and for our non-biological children and grandchildren to begin to name our roles in each other's lives and create deeper meaning and deeper sense of belonging to one another. These non-biological children may be deeply connected to our hearts in a variety of circumstances, including neighborhood children, youth and children in our church family, foster children, and youth or children we've been invited to mentor, instruct, or teach. This might also include children of divorce and remarriage. Whatever the circumstances, having terms to connect us to those people in our lives has the potential for creating *family* with one another.

These categories of distinction also serve the church community as a means of re-envisioning how the church might do ministry between generations. These definitions of family as *structural* and *functional* complement one another and provide keys for understanding families in our North American culture (Garland, 2012, 66).

Ultimately, these definitions of family give us a better understanding of what it means to be a grandparent in the twenty-first-century paradigm and such definitions are equally important for the way the church functions in the cultural reality of today's world. As Garland makes clear,

> [M]ost family ministries [in the local church] have been conceptualized using a structural definition of family. Therefore, we have ministry with married couples, with parents, with single parents, with single adults, with empty-nest couples and so on. No doubt, these ministries have been helpful to families dealing with various life-stage issues. On the other hand, this structural approach tends to cut a congregation into chunks of homogenous groups, so that all married couples are grouped for ministry, and all the singles, and so on. It also has the tendency toward congregational specialization, so that some congregations become known as the congregation for young families, or for single adults, or for senior adults. Inevitably, some types of families do not find specialized ministry for them, because most congregations do not have enough specialized staff and other resources to maintain a host of specialized ministries for the diversity of family types included in the congregation. Perhaps even more problematic is that families are deprived of relationships with others of different ages and life experiences, and the image of an inclusive community of all kinds of people—the people of God—is lost. (Garland, 2012, 66)

In light of these definitions of family, in recent years there has been a call for churches to rethink the ways in which they do ministry across the board and to rethink who fits into the category of *family*. A movement, which is becoming a mantra among many in current church leadership and which I predict will change the staff structure in many churches in the first half of the twenty-first century, is toward what is being referred to as *intergenerational* ministry or *messy church* (see for example, Allen and Ross, 2012, or Parsley, 2012).

I predict churches will move away from hiring specialized staff members who focus on ministry under a *structural* definition of *family*. Hiring for positions such as family pastors, ministers of youth, children, single, adult, and the like will morph into hiring staff for the purpose of serving with intergenerational teams or network teams that partner toward bringing generations together in forms that recognize a more *functional* reality of what the church looks like as the family of God, rather than offering only age- and stage-specific ministries.

THE GRAND-PARENTING EFFECT

That is fine for church staff, but why should this matter to grandparents?

> *We live in a world in which we need to share responsibility. It's easy to say, "It's not my child, not my community, not my world, not my problem." Then there are those who see the need and respond. I consider those people my heroes.* —Spoken in 1994, quoted in Fred Rogers' obituary in the *Pittsburgh Post-Gazette*

I write about this *churchy* stuff because I believe it is important for those of grandparenting age to realize that this shift in the ways the church and church programs are run in our culture is impacted by the views held by all generations in the church. I write this final chapter because I believe that in God's economy there is no such thing as other people's children. Although change is slow, churches are becoming more aware of the need for generations to speak into the lives of each other and this is very good news if you care to be in a position of influence in your church community. It is also good news if you have ever felt alienated from your children or your grandchildren's generations *even in your church community*, and especially if you are among the current grandparent generation who have experienced having your children or grandchildren leave to attend a church they felt was more relevant to their particular demographic needs. It is also good news for considering the potential role you might play in the lives of younger people in your congregation as churches move toward intergenerational forms of ministry.

The key point to this final chapter in a book on the grandparenting effect is that you might begin to see your role as being *functional* grandparents for members of younger generations even if they are not *structurally* related to you. I want to encourage you to practice thinking outside the current cultural box that was created over the past few decades and begin to reimagine your potential for influence in the lives of various biologically related or non-biologically related young people.

THE GRANDPARENTING EFFECT ON NON-BIOLOGICAL GRANDCHILDREN

Love is the greatest need in our church families
. . . and in our neighborhoods

Modeling is the chief way children are trained. Kids take our worst characteristics as parents and multiply them by a factor of ten. I've heard it said that what one generation tolerates, the next generation will exaggerate. Love is the great need in our church families. But it must start with those who are older. Culture is passed on through the actions, attitudes, and opportunities that the leaders of a church embrace.
Our kids learn to love us because we've spent so much time loving them.
—Ross Parsley, *Messy Church*

Too often it seems that churches in western culture have morphed into a service providing institution more than seeing themselves in the role of being family of God together. There is actually a term for this, it is called *familying* (Going, 2014, vibrantfaith.org). *Familying* is an action verb, a process of becoming meaningful participants in the lives of others rather than coming together just for what we feel we will get out of it. When you are familying, you don't ask yourself, *I wonder who's preaching today* before you decide if you should go to church. An attitude of *familying* shifts the focus from us and our felt needs to a desire to encourage others and develop meaningful relationships with others. It is a recognition that God intends us—the church—to *family* one another. And when we look back at the story of Abraham and Sarah and the reality of being invited into God's covenant family (see chapter one), we begin to see the biblical story from beginning to end and realize that the church does not exist to fix us or our families; the church exists to invite us to be part of God's story, God's *functional* family.

I have a friend who is always asking, "Are you feeling me here?" So, are you? Are you feeling the privileges and responsibilities of being a grandparent not only with biological grandchildren but potentially with other youth and children in the church and the community? It is a great privilege to look for opportunities to grandparent the church's children and see them as our *grandchildren-in-faith*. It is a great privilege to be a part of bringing generations together in meaningful ways of creating belonging. Of course, this works best when the whole church catches the vision. So, what can you do right now to set an example and move toward *familying* some *grandchildren-in-faith*? Here are a couple of stories of what this looks like.

THE GRAND-PARENTING EFFECT

Invitations for mentoring, modeling, and creating functional family

A favorite story on the role of non-biological grandparents willing to step in the gap and become mentors and models was shared with me by my friend, Paul Martin, who awhile back, due in part to my meddling in his life, found himself as the new CEO of Royal Family Kids, an international organization that creates positive, life-changing moments for innocent children who have been victims of neglect, abuse, and abandonment. After Paul's first Royal Family Kids Camp he wrote this about becoming a Royal Family grandparent:

> There are two older couples at Royal Family Kids Camp. They are the camp *Grandmas and Grandpas*. [They come to spend this week at camp with these kids] because many of these children, given they have no parents, have no grandparents. And as many of you know, grandparents can be a very good thing for children.
>
> I wouldn't be who I am today without the remarkable influence of my grandparents. So, one of the camp activities include grandma and grandpa. We take our kids into a room—ten of them, just boys. We sit on a chair in a semicircle. We are facing the two couples, the *grandparents*. They are in front of a fireplace. They are older and married.
>
> The kids are squeamish, as always. The grandparents introduce themselves, not as *Bob* or *Mary*, or *Mr. Thompson* and *Mrs. Thompson*, but as *Grandpa Bob* and *Grandma Mary*. As they speak, you can see that the objective is to model kindness, calm, wisdom—something of which children see very little.
>
> They gently, with such calm and patience, make eye contact and [invite] the children to listen. I'm inside so I can't wear my sunglasses but tears stream down my face because I'm sure these children have never experienced anything like this; they act out, and these older authority figures gently steer them in the right direction.
>
> *I hate that I can sometimes be so emotional. I got it from my maternal grandfather, my Nonno. He was strong and gruff and full of life, and he cried whenever the circumstances warranted it.* You could see the children being calmed.

One of the grandmas begins to read them a story. She sits and reads and shows them the pictures. It's a story about a boy, named Denver, who grew up a slave in the deep south. Later [Denver] ran away to a big city. He became homeless. He was illiterate. He had no family. He became angry because he *wasn't like the other people.*

Grandma gently told the children, with poise and grace, how sadness can turn to anger when life is hard. All implication, no sermon, nothing about their respective circumstances. The twenty eyes fixed on grandma with each word.

The story ends with a [family] reaching out to Denver. They teach him to read. They love him. He becomes a responsible and respectful member of society because he chooses to not let sadness and anger rule him. He starts an outreach to the homeless. He is honored in the White House by President Obama.

And the moral of the book is about how we are all uniquely different, and nobody is better than someone else.

One of the grandpas takes out his Taylor guitar. He sings a cheesy song about a father's love. *I'm cringing a bit; the kids aren't. I keep thinking about how these kids live on video games and smartphones and here are these four old people singing this cheesy song and how it's not relevant.* Apparently, it was. Because the [kids] are paying full attention.

The song ends. Then the grandpa says, "I've never known my dad. I never met him. I don't know his name or what he looks like."

I cry some more.

Four hands are raised. He calls on one of the boys who says, "Me too." Then I hear three others say "me too." One says, "I know my father's name. His name is Richard. And I have a picture of him. But I've never met him."

The grandpa who doesn't know his father then talks with such precision and grace about how God is a father that will never let us down. One boy talks about how parents can let us down but "if you trust in God he never leaves us."

I don't even know how the Grandparent time ended. But after it did, one of the camp photographers (there are a few of them) asked the boys if they wanted to have a picture taken with "your new grandparents." The cynic in me (I'm sorry to admit this) immediately said, "These cool, hardened customers are not going to want a picture taken with these old white folks."

One of the grandmas pointed to me—as a mob rushed to be first in line—to help navigate the photo session. I had to find a way to back them up so the shoot could begin.

One after one, the boys sat on a chair, with each grandparent couple to his left and right.

The smiles of the boys. We can't show pictures of them. But those smiles. They will never leave my heart.

The grandfather in the mix: mentoring, modeling, and creating functional family

Another story is about Uncle Louie. I had recently taken a new ministry position at a large church in Southern California which offered lots of programming for a large population of children and youth. After my previous position with a smaller congregation in Illinois, this felt a bit overwhelming. There were so many layers of policies and guidelines on what we could or couldn't do. There were forms to be filled out by parents, and official protection policies and permission slips. In this mix I encountered Uncle Louie, who volunteered rather unofficially with our junior highers. Louie would show up at Wednesday evening youth group and just hang out with the kids. And I noticed that the kids loved him even as some of the adult leaders in the room cringed. The junior high youth pastor at that time has written a story about Uncle Louie for this book, which you will find in the bridge section following this chapter. As I reflect back on those days I realize all the cultural taboos that were breached. For starters, I am actually not sure to this day if Louie ever completed a background check, which was required to work with children and youth in that church. Here was Louie, a man, a grandfather with grown children and biological grandchildren that lived in another state. We in church ministry live in fear that we will be responsible for a pedophile harming our kids and red flags often go up when older men volunteer; however, the reality is that the majority of grandpa-aged men are not a danger to our kids. Should or should we not be more careful? What might our youth be losing by our cultural fears of older men and stranger danger? I wonder if perhaps the greatest loss is that both grandpas and the kids lose out when fear and protocol take over.

We in the church, and in the community in general, too often communicate the message that older (or single) men are not welcome unless it is in areas such as sports and coaching. Even the research I study on grandparenting admits that most of the information comes from the role of grandmothers, not grandfathers (for example: Arber and Timonen, 2012). What might it mean for grandfathers to be welcomed, included, and embraced as mentors, models, and *grandfathers-in-faith* (aka functional grandfathers) for our youth in the church and community? One of the biggest hurdles might be getting men of this age to realize the gift they have to offer.

That was the gift that Uncle Louie was to our junior highers. I was pleased to welcomed Mr. Rol into our children's ministry, one who *did* complete a background check. Rol was also a biological grandfather and had served the church in many capacities over his life, including a term or more on the church board and as a member of the Christian education committee. He signed up to teach third graders at Vacation Bible School (VBS) one summer. I partnered him with a single mother, which turned out to be a win/win. Not only was he in a position to mentor the children, but he also serendipitously served as a mentor and grandfather figure to that single mother. After that week of VBS, Rol and that mother signed on as a teaching team in Sunday school, showing up to teach during Saturday evening services, and then showing up for worship with his wife on Sunday mornings. He continued to teach Sunday school and VBS as long as he was mentally and physically able and became a special gift to our church's third graders for nearly a decade, not only in a teaching capacity but greeting children in the church plaza or in worship and showing up for our third grade Bible presentation brunches.

Another story is that of the *man cave*, which in this case refers to a very large space in a local assisted living facility near our home in Southern California. This space was created as a workroom where men moving into the facility could bring their tools and spend as much time as they desired tinkering on model railroads and airplanes, woodworking projects, and the like. It is quite an impressive space! At some point along the way one of the older men invited one of the staff's children to come work on the model railroad and soon it became a formal benefit of working on staff to have your kids invited to show up at the man cave to work on projects with the older men. This serendipitously became an opportunity for mentoring and modeling and teaching useful skills to the youth. It seems to me that this is an easy model to replicate in other assisted living facilities, if only someone has the vision.

I was recently invited to visit the Assistance League chapter in Laguna Beach, California, which, way back in 1976, began providing an *early intervention program* in collaboration with professional therapists. This EIP provides weekly family-centered therapy sessions and specialized services for children age one and under who have been identified as at risk or diagnosed with conditions known to cause developmental delays. This is an excellent program with one of the most meaningful parts being a group of grandparenting age adults who volunteer to show up and rock the babies for an hour or so every week, allowing the parents some much needed respite and community education time. As expected, most of the grandparent rockers are women; however, I discovered that there was at least one grandfather in the mix. It is such a simple opportunity to bless one another. That grandfather's story is written in his own words in the bridge following this chapter.

We all need mentors, models, and meaning-makers in our lives

I have discovered and valued the influence of older and wiser and *R.E.&A.L.* people in my own life over the years. Perhaps this is partly because my parents married and had children relatively late in life. As I mentioned before, my parents were forty-one and forty-five when I was born, so I never got to know my own grandparents. My mother's parents had both died by the time I was two years of age. I have sweet memories of going out to my father's childhood home in Darling, Mississippi when I was younger than three. Perhaps that memory comes more from old family pictures of me on that farm than they come from actually being there. However, I do remember that my grandmother was old and sick and we were taken into her room one or two at a time so as not to overwhelm her. I sat on the edge of her bed as my father prayed over her; I was no more than four, maybe younger. My paternal grandfather must have died shortly after that—I honestly don't remember. All this is to communicate to you, my dear readers, that from an early age

THE GRANDPARENTING EFFECT ON NON-BIOLOGICAL GRANDCHILDREN

I learned to value the influence of *functional* grandmothers, grandfathers, aunts, and uncles in my life, mostly in my church life. Perhaps you want or need to take a moment now to stop reading, close your eyes, and recall those who could be considered *functional* family in your own life.

> We all need grandmothers, grandfathers, aunts, uncles, cousins, and friends, if they are available. If they are not available, we need to create a home with trusted people on our own. We might meet them in church or in some other group. We need wise surrogates for kin, who may be absent or inappropriate, to help with the struggles and to celebrate the pleasures of family life. Trusted friends, who are older and from outside the family have an authority different from a parent's which is sometimes needed in families. (Berryman, 2018, 124–25)

The most advantageous way to raise children is by surrounding them with a system of caregivers that provide the children and their parents with love and support. As has been pointed out, this type of system is sometimes called alloparenting, and involves situations where several people are involved in caring for a child besides the child's biological parents (Hrdy, 2011). Research suggests that the greater the number of close and caring relationships one has, the better the person's health and well-being will be throughout life (e.g., Feeney and Collins, 2014). This research is also supported by the extended and ongoing research of The Search Institute in Minnesota, which publishes current research on developmental assets. It has been confirmed by numerous studies that the most impactful ministry with youth in a church setting is not to give them a state-of-the-art youth facility, nor to hire an amazing new youth director; but rather to surround them with adults other than their parents that will speak into their lives. This is reason enough to claim that the best ministry is to place youth in an ongoing context of intergenerational worship, education, and mission. When a congregation, for example, plans a summer mission trip to build houses in a needy community, they enrich the experience for the youth by recruiting several adults, including senior adult men, who will go along. It is also advantageous to recruit young families with small children to join the mission team so the experience is also enhanced by the connection between the teens and younger children. In other words, research shows us the value of generations—not necessarily biologically related—in making a positive difference in the lives of everyone involved. So if you are a grandparent or of grandparent age, be prepared to say "yes" when your church's youth leaders come to you with a request to serve on the youth mission team next summer. Better yet, you might want to consider the role of Uncle Louis or Mr. Rol or that of one of the other stories shared in this chapter or in the bridge following the chapter.

The practical role of intergenerational music
—it's good for us all

The final story in the bridge following this chapter comes from my friend Jennifer Boles. I first met Jennifer when she served on my staff as our preschool music teacher. It was not long before Jennifer asked if she could begin offering a music program with a Down Syndrome organization. She set this up for Wednesday afternoons when Down Syndrome children would attend with their parents. From there I watched Jennifer move further and further into what has become her career and her passion in life, to connect generations with the gift of music. When I asked Jennifer for information on her passion she told me that she could write a book on the practical benefits of music for all generations. I believe that one of these days she will do just that; however, for the purpose of this book and for you as a grandparent, here's a summary of benefits my friend Jennifer lists about experiencing music with children and youth.

- *Music meets sociocultural & spiritual need.* The number of adults over the age of sixty-five in our society is on track to double within the next twenty years, a phenomenon referred to as the *Silver Tsunami*. For many of us seniors, the passing of a loved one leaves us on our own; this might even be the case in your life. In such cases, seniors find themselves longing for companionship and community. On the other hand, our society is filled with an increasing number of parents with young children who find themselves balancing full-time careers while they seek opportunities for providing quality childcare and school options. All of this is taking place while members from both generations often live countries and cultures apart from their biological family roots. It is because seniors bring an understanding of life experience and mentorship that our young families desire time with them. So, a robust intergenerational program of grandparent-aged persons and grandchildren is just the answer, and according to Jennifer's research, music is just the tool to make this magic happen.

- *Music is like a neurological uber vitamin.* Music ignites all areas of brain development and strengthening, including intellectual, social-emotional, motor, language, and overall literacy, by helping the body and the mind work together. Music is relational in nature between one note to another, therefore, this architectural and mathematical structure invites our brains to make sense of it in a powerful way. The rhythmic and melodic patterns provide exercise for the brain and help develop and maintain memory by activating both sides of the brain. Music engages the brain while stimulating the neural pathways that are associated with higher forms of intelligence as abstract thinking, empathy, and mathematics. Learning the ABCs with the ABC song is a perfect example! While grandparent and grandchild are laughing, singing, dancing, and having fun, new neurons and synapses are forming and strengthening for both generations.

- *Music encourages socially responsible behaviors.* Music, music education, and music therapy nurtures confidence, coordination, concentration, and persistence while teaching young children how to listen, follow directions, take turns, and participate with each of their peers and other adults beyond the biological family unit. As I wrote about back in chapter five, Seattle's Providence Mount St. Vincent nursing home also houses a childcare center. One of the activities the grandparents and children do together is make music.

  Developmentally appropriate music activities involve the whole child—the child's desire for language, the body's urge to move, the brain's attention to patterns, the ear's lead in initiating communication, the voice's response to sounds, as well as the eye-hand coordination associated with fine and large motor activities. We never lose the need to keep our brains strong and maintain our proficiencies with these skills, so when grandchild and grandparent are both learning and teaching and leading each other while engaging in these developmentally appropriate activities, they are becoming more proficient and the minds of both seniors and young children grow and develop.

- *Music is multisensory.* Grandchildren with special needs often learn in different ways and grandparents with cognitive issues need reinforcement. Creatively playing music engages them in tactile, kinesthetic, auditory, and visual learning/reinforcement with each other. Additionally, for both grandchild and grandparent, where language and/or emotional expression is difficult, singing and playing simple instruments together provides that safe space to be successful with expression in a fun and joyful way!

- *Music evokes singing and physical movement.* Both grandparent and grandchild delight in this emotional expression of God's love for us and one another. According to Jennifer Boles, whether we are learning new songs or singing favorites that span generations, a bond of caring and security is established within this intergenerational community. Both secular and sacred music is marked by balance, color, texture, and harmony that draws us into the world that God created, as it draws us to each other.

Ultimately, this deep sense of beauty and belonging draw us closer to God, as we realize, grandparent and grandchild alike, that we are all God's children and belong together whether biologically related in *structural* family or related as *functional* family. This is an area where churches must get creative if they are to grow meaningfully in our segmented and separated society of the twenty-first century. When I talk with my friend Jennifer and read her story, when I consider the model of such facilities as Seattle's Providence Mount St. Vincent nursing home and childcare center, I am encouraged for the church as we move in meaningful ways into the future.

Bridge 8: Stories of Becoming Family for One Another

*Personal stories from people who become family
in all walks of life and in nontraditional ways*

Seeking to walk in His footsteps: Remembering Heritage House . . . *by Ruth Lampe*

A few years ago I was one of the Bible leader volunteers from our church for young women at Heritage House in Costa Mesa, California. It was a difficult and challenging opportunity to bring the Word and the love of Jesus to these young women, many mothers of young children. The judicial system allowed them to serve some of their prison time in this homemaking environment and this time with their children.

Many of these women came from a generation of families that knew nothing of Jesus Christ so they had nothing growing up that would lead them on the path to Jesus. This is where I found it so difficult. Not in sharing my love for Jesus but that I felt I would never be able to relate until I perhaps had a history of robbing a 7-Eleven store.

How foolish was my fear. Jesus walked in that classroom with me and it was a blessing for me. We sat around a large table, about twelve young women, along with support leaders. As I began, with my Bible open in front of me, all was quiet as I said, "Today, because you are a new group, I would like to begin with each one of you, asking you to share how you stand with Jesus." Quiet continued as they sat with closed Bibles in front of them, a gift from our church. I turned to the young woman on my left and said, "Let's begin with you." And I repeated the question.

Quietly she said, "I don't know that name." I felt pain—how can that be? In depth of feeling, I turned to her again and said, "And you probably have never heard about eternal life either, have you?" She quietly said, "No."

Composing myself, leaning not on my own wisdom, I went to each young women with the same question. Their answers were similar: "I have seen that name on a bumper sticker"; "my grandmother knows Jesus and I want to get clean for her." Another said, "I see that book in front of me, but I don't know what I would even do with it if I opened it, or what would I look for?"

Can you see how hard it was for me? I don't know people that don't know my Jesus. How can that be? Are we keeping this precious knowledge to just a few? How we fail you, Lord.

There came a time a few months later that I sadly shared with these women—some of them we saw changes in—that I found it so hard because I did not share their history and didn't know if I was the right person to lead this Bible study. The girls responded that they loved me and shared this. "We look at you like our Grandmother. Please don't stop coming!"

Lord, help me to remember it was not easy for you or for your disciples. We just have to keep our eyes on you and tell others about you, knowing that the Spirit of Our Lord is with us. Let us not fail in this.

BRIDGE 8: STORIES OF BECOMING FAMILY FOR ONE ANOTHER

*Heritage House opened in June of 1992 as the first women and children's residential treatment facility in Orange County. The six-month program has a static capacity of sixteen adults and twenty children. Heritage House provided needs assessment, case management and service linkage, individual and group counseling, peer support groups, substance abuse/HIV/STD/ life skills education, parenting skills classes, and sober social activities for mothers and their children. Although now closed, Heritage House was the agency's first Orange County program, leading the way for Heritage House North, Heritage House Village, and Heritage House Cottages—all serving substance-addicted women and their children.

The Story of Mr. Magic and the Baby Whisperer
. . . by David FarFar Carlson

Back in the mid-1980s an alarming article appeared in the *Detroit Free Press*. It was a report of a sudden decline in volunteers at the Detroit Medical Center's infant wards. This sudden decline, it seems, was due to a new mandate that HIV-positive babies could not be identified as to their condition because doing so would violate the confidentiality of the mother. This came about very early in the HIV scare, when many people—including the medical center's volunteers—falsely assumed that HIV could be caught from an HIV-positive infant. It was about that time that I began volunteering during the dinner hour every Tuesday. I continued for several years.

The rewards of volunteering in the infant wards were astounding. Parents of hospitalized infants assumed that when they came to visit their babies they would likely find them alone and often crying; however, the expressions on the faces of parents was both memorable and priceless as they entered a hospital room in which I, as a volunteer, was holding their infants in a rocking chair. I was able to serve those infants and their parents this way for more than six years. I was nicknamed "Mr. Magic" because I would walk down a corridor, hear an infant in distress, and quickly calm him or her before moving on down the hall to comfort the next infant in distress.

After relocating from Michigan to California, I found a new opportunity for volunteering in a program sponsored by the Assistance League of Laguna

Beach. This program is unique and operates until the title, Early Intervention Program (EIP). It provides a weekly family-centered therapy sessions and specialized services for children identified as at risk or diagnosed with conditions known to cause developmental delays. Each week, babies and their parents move through several stations that emphasize improving cognitive and occupational skills. After the infants complete these stations, parents bring them to us. We are mostly grandparent-age adults who volunteer to rock the infants while their parents engage in discussions related to raising and nurturing their special needs child. It is in this setting that I have been flattered with the new nickname, the "Baby Whisperer."

Between these two volunteering experiences, in my personal life I lost an infant granddaughter who died at childbirth. However, I have realized that my participation in these programs has little or nothing to do with this loss; rather it has been driven by an intuitive and compelling need to connect with and nurture these infants. As a religious humanist I have not only benefited greatly from being able to participate in these programs, but it also helps fulfill my commitment to improving the human condition, even in a small way.

The Story of Uncle Louie . . . *by Ivan Klaussen*

Uncle Louie came to me when I was a youth minister in 2003. He had decided to be a junior high volunteer. We soon began calling him Uncle Louie . . . because that's exactly what he was, an uncle-like figure to our junior highers as well as to our ministry leaders.

Louie was born in 1933, so he was seventy at the time. He loved just being *with* the kids and had no magic tricks or whatever to captivate them. Uncle Louie had zero hidden agendas nor did he have a hero complex that so often plagues youth volunteers. Unlike some of our youth volunteers, he needed no community service hours! He simply enjoyed the role of Uncle Louie. He would regale the kids with stories of how he had invented sonar or would recite Lewis Carroll's poem, "The Jabberwocky." The kids—and I mean all the kids—got a total kick out of him.

Louie read somewhere that kids would always pay attention to the oldest person in the room if they authentically paid attention to them, and that is just what Uncle Louie did. He was faithful and showed up to everything! I mean every Wednesday youth group, every week for Sunday School, every all-nighters and even Winter and Summer Camp. He never skipped a beat, never got angry, and he spouted off Scripture with exegetical ease. He was even-keeled and loved Jesus in front of those kids. He was not perfect nor would he have ever claimed to have been. He was just Uncle Louie who even when explaining *red shift* to these thirteen- and fourteen-year-old teens, did it as though they had already spent two years in advance biochemistry classes at Harvard.

Uncle Louie was one of the most incredible volunteers I have ever encountered because he loved authentically and unapologetically in both his relationship to Jesus Christ and to those junior high kids. Uncle Louie was one of a kind in our church ministry; but thanks be to God for all the *Uncle Louies* who are dappled throughout Youth Ministries across the world!

A Story of Rhythm and Relationship and Creating Sacred Space
. . . by Jennifer Boles

Nearly twenty-five years ago, I had the privilege of being introduced to teaching music and movement to parents and their children. The fun and joy continued while directing one of the largest early childhood music and movement programs in the country for ten years, where many little ones had autism or Down Syndrome. Flash forward many years later, and I found myself working in the field of senior health care, where I experienced the same joy by incorporating music and movement with new families with loved ones diagnosed with dementia or Alzheimer's disease in addition to those with Parkinson's and other forms of Mild Cognitive Impairment (MCI).

With these experiences at both ends of the generational spectrum, I was blessed to witness the power of music in creating a magical space for physical, mental/emotional, and spiritual development. I witnessed the power of music to both draw them out of themselves and draw them together in sacred belonging!

There is a unique and beautiful element in the arts, music in particular, that nurtures the spiritual connectedness between generations of grandparents and grandchildren, of old and young. A spiritual musical environment is both a reflection of God's love, and an inspiration to the entire community.

In my work I have had the joy of seeing the rich gift of connecting and belonging that music gives—especially across generations. Music is the lifeblood of generational connection that passes on long-standing family traditions and history. Music creates a sense of agency and identity of self within a particular community and family. Along with many others in my profession, I have observed that singing and making simple rhythmic instrumental music is a powerful way for generations at both ends of the spectrum to come to understand and process information, express themselves, and connect with the world around them.

This work with music and generational connection has been a gift in my life and a joy to bring to my professional work. I am currently working on a grant proposal for the use of music in bringing senior health care together with a cultural need for more and better quality childcare and schooling options for young families.

My work is to create a space where generations come together to meet sociocultural and spiritual needs; a space that involves the expression of feelings through singing, instrumentation, and even dance. Since children often do not have the words to express themselves and need positive ways to release their emotions, seniors (whether biological grandparents or others of that generation) provide the much-needed listening and affirmation, and in turn, receive an increased sense of self-esteem and decreasing sense of isolation.

Additionally, as we age, we often recall the faith traditions of our most formative years (birth through five years). This developmental journey crosses all faith traditions and includes prayers and songs. Recent research shows that even with significant memory loss, music that we learn during our early years and throughout our life journey is stored deep within our brain. This salient part of our brain is not touched, keeping musical memory alive. We see this regularly when we have three-year-olds and eighty-three-year olds singing "Jesus Loves Me" or "Frere Jacque (Are You Sleeping, Brother

BRIDGE 8: STORIES OF BECOMING FAMILY FOR ONE ANOTHER

John)." Grandchild is learning and grandparent is recalling! Music transmits culture and is an avenue by which beloved songs, rhymes, and dances can be passed down from one generation to another.

By celebrating the simplest songs and stories, a grandparent is reminded of, and likewise helps a little one to discover that they both *belong* in an ongoing story and have a special place in their own family, and this new extended family of community, regardless of age or ability.

A Church's Guide to Bringing Generations Together

Why add a section on a *church's guide to bringing generations together* in a book addressed to grandparents? As I wrote in the introduction, this is a book not only for grandparents and grandparent-age adults, it is also a book for the church community to begin to think seriously about how to bring generations together. In doing so, grandparents are in a better position to connect and engage with younger generations in the church community as well as with their own biological grandchildren. Better yet, when the church becomes a generationally equipping community, not only do members discover the richness of doing life and ministry side by side, the younger generations grows stronger and everyone begins to find their places of belonging in God's ancient-future story. So I encourage you, if you are on ministry staff at a church *or* if you are a grandparent with influence over your church's governing body, to consider this brief list of suggestions geared toward engaging the grandparenting effect on non-biological grandchildren in your church community.

1. ***Re-member* generations in your community by telling the story to which all Christian communities belong**

    Warren Cole Smith, in celebration of the birthdays of well loved storytellers C. S. Lewis and Madeleine L'Engle, pointed out that "stories shape our imaginations—stories teach us what is true. If you can control the stories a people see, hear, and tell each other, you can ultimately control what they think and even how they think" (Smith,

2018) and, Bartholomew and Goheen write that "all human communities live out some story that provides a context for understanding the meaning of history and gives shape and direction to their lives. If we allow the Bible to become fragmented, we are in danger of being absorbed into whatever other story is shaping our culture, and the Scripture and heritage will thus cease to shape our lives as it should" (Bartholomew and Goheen, 2004, 12). By telling the Bible as God's story we are engaged in the realization that we belong to something bigger and deeper and older than right here and right now. Our ancestors in faith have much to teach us about trusting God, and most of them did not belong to a *traditional family* by twentieth-century standards.

2. ***Re-member* generations in your community by looking at *all* of your church planning and ministry through the *lens* of intergenerational community**

   Even churches that try to be intergenerational in their ministry still have a tendency to look at ministry through a *siloed* perspective and plan ministry accordingly for specific age or stage demographic. The trick is to form staff in such a way that they are put into positions of visioning and planning with staff overseeing other departments. Of course, when you think about it, having your church divided up by demographics or departments with staff hired specifically for such areas puts you at a disadvantage from the start. The most effective way to allow your church to truly begin to plan *intergenerationally* is to stop hiring *youth directors, children's directors, adult formation directors, even family pastors* . . . Instead begin hiring and recruiting *intergenerational teams.* Then on that team you can assign areas of focus while keeping the vision integrated.

3. ***Re-member* generations in your community by worshiping together in community (not just once a year or even once a month)**

   Perhaps a biblical study on worship as a church staff and/or as a community-wide Bible study focus is a great place to begin. There are many great book studies on worshiping in community, in the bibliography of this book, to get you started, see specifically books titled *Intergenerational Faith Formation: Bringing the Whole Church Together in Ministry, Community and Worship* (Allen and Ross, 2012),

BRIDGE 8: STORIES OF BECOMING FAMILY FOR ONE ANOTHER

and *Story-Shaped Worship: Following Patterns from the Bible and History* by Robbie Castleman (whose story appears in the bridge section following chapter five).

4. ***Re-member* generations in your community by creating intergenerational small groups or sacred suppers *with* mixed ages**

When all ages come together for fellowship or small group gatherings, especially over a meal together, all benefit from hearing each other's stories and experiences. Even the way we understand and apply Scripture in Bible study is enhanced by intergenerational understanding and wisdom, even the wisdom of the youngest member of the group, when they are invited to contribute. A favorite story is from my friend, Holly Allen (author of several books, including *Intergenerational Faith Formation: Bringing the Whole Church Together in Ministry, Community and Worship*). In a chapter she authored for Robert Keeley's book *Shaped By God: Twelve Essentials for Nurturing Faith in Children, Youth and Adults,* Holly shares this story from an intergenerational small group in which she participated:

The icebreaker question in our intergenerational small group was *when you daydream or imagine, what do you see yourself doing?* Among the responses were these:

- I see myself in college, loving it, having a boyfriend. (Jennifer, a teen)
- I like to imagine myself as an NFL quarterback, winning the Super Bowl! (Kevin, forty-something)
- I'm in the World Series and I hit a home run with bases loaded in the bottom of the ninth and win the game! (Chris, a graduate student)
- I'm always a Ninja Turtle. (Nolan, a fourth grader)
- I'm back in Vietnam, saving the buddies in my platoon. (Carlos, sixty-something)
- I imagine Ben living with us again; he has a good job. We have another baby, a girl. (Jan, thirty-something)

The it was Cora's turn. Cora is eighty-something; Charlie, her husband of fifty-five years, died a decade ago. She whispers, "I imagine myself in heaven with Jesus; Charlie is there, James [her deceased son] is there, my mother and dad and my sister, Robbie, are there, and then our other children start to join us, and then, their children. And it just goes on and on. I greet each one with open arms and homemade cookies!"

There was a quiet pause. Then Nolan said, "I'll be there too." Jennifer said, "Me too."

And everyone joined in. (Allen, in Keeley, ed., 2010, 125)

5. ***Re-member* generations in your community by producing together**

Major benefits arise from inviting all generations to serve and go on short-term mission opportunities together. Youth learn skills from grandparent age, small children are mentored by teenage youth, and everyone develops a strong sense of belonging in community when they have produced something of worth side by side. When generations work together they learn from and encourage one another. In an era that places value on consumerism, producing something together creates deeper meaning and relationship.

Appendix

When this book was only a twinkle in my eye, a tickle in my brain, and a passion in my heart, a friend in ministry asked for advice. Below is her note and my reply, which I hope might be helpful to you as a grandparent, a minister, or a friend. (Please note: the book lists are by no means exhaustive!)

My friend's note to me:

I reach out to you because I know you to be an intentional grandparent in sharing your faith with your own grandchildren. I have had a grandmother within our church ask if she and her husband could meet with me for counsel on how to share their love of Jesus with their grandchildren. The grandchildren are unchurched and live out of town.

Although I have suggestions and some resources, I'd love to hear from you, who is actually in the season of grandparenting!

Ideas on any of the following would be helpful:

- *What are some favorite traditions, rituals, rhythms that you may have established?*
- *Do you have any favorite books or resources about grandparenting and faith?*
- *Favorite books, stories you read with your grandchildren?*
- *How do you introduce your grandchildren to Jesus when your children may not be doing so in their home?*
- *Any other words of wisdom?*

I value your insight in passing our faith to the generations to come.

APPENDIX

My reply to my friend:

What are some favorite traditions, rituals, rhythms that you may have established?

- If children were baptized as infants, find out the date and send them "Baptism Anniversary" cards each year on the date—I usually include a picture from their baptism day—even the same one every year is okay.

- Pronouncing blessings over your grands: there are several ways to do this, as simple as placing a hand on head or shoulder and saying: "May you always know how very much you are loved by me and loved by God." For another example, when we finished FaceTiming (or Skyping) with our grands when they were preschool age, I always put my index fingers together and they recognize this as a sign to get ready to sing "Go Now in Peace" together. And after a few times doing this, if I should forget, they would put their fingers together to remind me. (Note: this works most effectively with preschool-age grands.)

- At our house, no surprise, the girls love when I bring out the parable box or desert box and tell a story on the kitchen floor—usually early in the morning while their parents are still asleep. This is easy for anyone to do using Jerome Berryman's new book, *Stories of God at Home* (see bibliography).

- Reading together is definitely a tradition at our house, and when they were younger I read to them via FaceTime (which their mom *loved* because it kept them engaged for a while!). I sometimes brought out my copy of *Jesus Storybook Bible* and my granddaughter would run to get her copy and we'd open to the same page to read it together 2,500 miles apart.

- Rituals around dinnertime and holidays create special memories of visits with grandparents.

- We keep a Victorian dollhouse, that their Pops built for their mom, in our living room so it is always waiting for when they come to visit. (Who knows when playing dollhouse might open up an invitation to share faith? At least an opportunity to *wonder and imagine* together.)

APPENDIX

Do you have any favorite books or resources about grandparenting and faith?

- My newest book: *The Grandparenting Effect: Bridging Generations One Story at a Time*
- *Overcoming Grandparenting Barriers: How to Navigate Painful Problems with Grace and Truth,* by Larry Fowler.
- *Long Distance Grandparenting: Nurturing the Faith of Your Grandchildren When You Can't be there in Person,* by Wayne Rice.

Favorite books, stories you read with your grandchildren?

- *The Jesus Storybook Bible,* by Sally Lloyd-Jones
- *Stories of God at Home,* by Jerome Berryman (to read yourself and also to use the stories with grandchildren)
- *Imaginative Prayer: A Yearlong Guide for Your Child's Spiritual Formation,* by Jared Patrick Boyd
- *Common Prayer for Children and Families,* by Jenifer Gamber and Timothy Seamans
- *Baby Believer Board Books* from CatechesisBooks.com, by Danielle Hitchen and Jessica Blanchard

Books that open up discussions about compassion and understanding of others. There are so many that I could list! Here are just three true stories that have been adapted to children's picture books:

- *The Story of Ruby Bridges,* by Robert Coles and George Ford
- *Ruth and the Green Book,* by Calvin Alexander Ramsey, Gwen Strauss, and Floyd Cooper
- *Shooting at the Stars: the Christmas Truce of 1914,* by John Hendrix—story of the Christmas Truce during World War I.
- *Belle, the Last Mule at Gee's Bend: A Civil Rights Story,* by Calvin Alexander Ramsey & Bettye Stroud—presents in story form the reason why Dr. Martin Luther King Jr.'s casket was pulled by mules and what that had to do with the civil rights movement.
- *I Have a Dream,* excerpts from Dr. Martin Luther King Jr.'s famous speech with paintings by Kadir Nelson. Grade two and up, a beautiful visualization of Dr. King's speech and a great introduction for children.

APPENDIX

- *Psalm Twenty-Three,* illustrated by Tim Ladwig. Psalm 23 depicted in an urban neighborhood featuring black children over the course of a day.
- *Schomburg: The Man Who Built a Library,* by Carole Boston Weatherford. The incredible true story of the man who relentlessly researched and tracked down the histories, primary documents, prints, and all-but-lost books from and about the many black people who made contributions to art, science, freedom, government, and so on, even after his fifth grade teacher told him that black people had no history or heroes worth noting. His collection was bought by the Carnegie Corporation and is housed today in the 135th Street branch of the New York public library.

Read-aloud books for elementary children on faith and opening space for wondering. Again, there are so many that I could list! Here are just a few favorites:

- *The classics, of course, such as:*
  - *The Chronicles of Narnia* by C. S. Lewis
  - *At the Back of the North Wind; The Princess and Curdie; The Prince and the Goblin; The Wise Woman; Sir Gibbie;* plus others by George McDonald
  - *A Wrinkle in Time; The Wind in the Door; A Swiftly Tilting Planet;* plus the *Austin Family Chronicle Series* by Madeline L'Engle
- *Dangerous Journey: The Story of Pilgrim's Progress,* by Oliver Hunkin
- *The Rise and Fall of Mount Majestic,* by Jennifer Trafton
- *Paul Writes (a Letter),* by Chris Raschka
- *The Faithful Spy: The Story of Dietrich Bonhoeffer and the Plot to Kill Hitler,* by John Hendrix

Best elementary-age Bibles:

- *Adventure Bible* (NIV) from ZonderKIDS
- *English Standard Version (ESV) Youth Bible* from The Bible Society

APPENDIX

How to introduce your grandchildren to Jesus when your children may not be doing so in their home?

- Pray for them, talk freely and comfortably about prayer, and *let them know that you pray for them and why* . . . however,
  - Don't be pushy
  - Don't be judgmental
  - Don't be unnatural
- Create conversation space for wonder and questions that make it feel okay for them to ask questions. And learn to be comfortable and honest when you don't have all the answers
- Try using words like "I wonder" or "do you wonder why" or "imagine" when you ask questions
- Establish/recognize rituals and traditions in your home and your life and talk about them freely
- Read books with them and/or watch movies together and always seek to use these as springboards for conversations and imagination that opens up inviting and comfortable space for faith sharing. Remember that sharing your stories, your life, and your traditions with them is the most important gift you can give to them. Who knows when you'll be planting seeds that others may harvest or building bridges that they will want to cross over in their journey of life?

Any other words of wisdom?

I am attaching a few short grandparenting stories that friends have shared with me from their own experiences. (All the stories I include in this book are there because I think they might be encouraging to you and your friends. Please take time to read all of them in the bridges between the chapters of my book!)

Bibliography

Allen, Holly. "No Better Place." In *Shaped by God: Twelve Essentials for Nurturing Faith in Children, Youth, and Adults*, edited by John Keeley, 109–26. Grand Rapids: Faith Alive, 2010.
Allen, Holly, Ben Espinoza, and Trevecca Okholm. "Practicing Thankfulness with Children." *Intersections*, Fall 2015. https://www.lipscomb.edu/sites/default/files/2018-12/Enlightening%20the%20Eyes%20of%20our%20Heart.pdf.
Allen, Holly, and Christine Lawton Ross. *Intergenerational Faith Formation: Bringing the Whole Church Together in Ministry, Community, and Worship*. Downers Grove, IL: IVP Academic, 2012.
Arber, Sara, and Virpi Timonen. *Contemporary Grandparenting: Changing Family Relationships in Global Contexts*. UK: Policy, 2012.
Bartholomew, Craig G., and Michael W. Goheen. *The Drama of Scripture: Finding Our Place in the Biblical Story*. Grand Rapids: Baker, 2004.
Baumeister, Roy F., Jennifer D. Campbell, Joachim I. Krueger, and Kathleen D. Vohs. "Exploding the Self-Esteem Myth." *Scientific American* 292 (2005) 84–92.
Baumrind, Diane, et al. *Parenting for Character: Five Experts, Five Practices*. Washington, DC: csee, 2008.
Bengston, Vern, with Norella M. Putney and Susan Harris. *Families and Faith: How Religion Is Passed Down across Generations*. New York: Oxford University Press, 2013.
Berryman, Jerome W. "The Great Family" in *The Complete Guide to Godly Play®: Volume 2*, revised and expanded. New York: Church Publishing, 2017.
———. *Stories of God at Home: A Godly Play® Approach*. New York: Church Publishing, 2018.
Bolsinger, Tod. *It Takes a Church to Raise a Christian*. Grand Rapids: Brazos, 2004.
Borgo, Lacy Finn. *Spiritual Conversations with Children: Listening to God Together*. Downers Grove, IL: InterVarsity, 2020.
Boyd, Jared Patrick. *Imaginative Prayer: A Yearlong Guide for Your Child's Spiritual Formation*. Downers Grove: InterVarsity, 2017.
Bronson, Po, and Ashley Merryman. *NurtureShock: New Thinking About Children*. New York: Twelve, 2009.
Brown, Brené. "Brené Brown on Empathy." December 10, 2013. YouTube video, 2:53. https://www.youtube.com/watch?v=1Evwgu369Jw&feature=emb_title.
Brown, Carolyn. https://worshipingwithchildren.blogspot.com/.

BIBLIOGRAPHY

Carlson, Melody, Heather Kopp, and Linda Clare. *Lost Boys and the Moms Who Love Them: Help and Hope for Dealing with your Wayward Son*. Colorado Springs: WaterBrook, 2002.

Castleman, Robbie F. *Story Shaped Worship: Following Patterns from the Bible and History*. Downers Grove, IL: InterVarsity, 2013.

Cavanaugh, William T. *Being Consumed: Economics and Christian Desire*. Grand Rapids: Eerdmans, 2008.

Celtic Daily Prayer, books 1 and 2. The Northumbria Community Trust. New York: HarperCollins, 2015.

Chabon, Michael. "Manhood for Amateurs: The Pleasures and Regrets of a Husband, Father, and Son." *The New York Review of Books*, July 16, 2009. https://www.nybooks.com/articles/2009/07/16/manhood-for-amateurs-the-wilderness-of-childhood.

Cherlin, Andrew. "The Deinstitutionalization of American Marriage." *Journal of Marriage and Family* 66.4 (November 2004) 848–61.

Claiborne, Shane, Jonathan Wilson-Hartgrove, and Enuma Okoro. *Common Prayer: A Liturgy for Ordinary Radicals*. Grand Rapids: Zondervan, 2010.

Cloninger, C. R. *Feeling Good: The Science of Well-Being*. New York: Oxford University Press, 2004.

Coles, Robert, and George Ford. *The Story of Ruby Bridges: Special Anniversary Ed*. New York: Scholastic, 2010.

Connidis, Ingrid Arnet. *Family Ties and Aging*. Newbury Park, CA: Pine Forge, 2010.

Covey, Stephen. *The Seven Habits of Highly Effective Families*. New York: Golden, 1997.

Crook, Christina. *The Joy of Missing Out: Finding Balance in a Wired World*. Gabriola Island, BC: New Society, 2015.

DeNeff, Steve. *Seven Saving Graces: Living Above the Deadly Sins*. Indianapolis: Wesleyan, 2010.

Dillard, Annie. *Pilgrim at Tinker Creek*. New York: Harper Perennial, 1974.

Dweck, Carol. S. "Caution—Praise Can Be Dangerous." *American Educator* 23.1 (1999) 4–9.

Feeney, Brooke C., and Nancy L. Collins. "A New Look at Social Support: A Theoretical Perspective on Thriving Through Relationships." *SAGE Journal*, August 14, 2014, 113–47.

Finn-Borgo, Lacy. *Spiritual Conversations with Children: Listening to God Together*. Downers Grove, IL: InterVarsity, 2020.

Ford, Leighton. *The Attentive Life: Discerning God's Presence in All Things*. Downers Grove, IL: IVP, 2008.

Foster, Richard J. *Celebration of Discipline: The Path to Spiritual Growth*. San Francisco: Harper, 2002.

Fowler, Larry. *Overcoming Grandparenting Barriers: How to Navigate Painful Problems with Grace and Truth*. Minneapolis: Bethany House, 2019.

Fries, Kimberly. *Examination of Conscience for Little Ones*. Independently published. 2019.

———. *Lectio Divina for Little Ones*. Independently published. 2019.

Gamber, Jenifer, and Timothy J. S. Seamans. *Common Prayer for Children and Families*. New York: Church, 2020.

Garland, Diana. *Family Ministry: A Comprehensive Guide*. 2d ed. Downers Grove, IL: InterVarsity, 2012.

Going, Nancy. "Are You Familying?" www.vibrantfaith.org/2014/09/are-you-familying/.

BIBLIOGRAPHY

Godspacelight website. https://godspacelight.com/

Gross, Bobby. *Living the Christian Year: Time to Inhabit the Story of God*. Downers Grove, IL: InterVarsity, 2009.

Harding, Sharon. *Keeping Sabbath with Older Children*. UK: Circle, 2010.

Harris, Alexander. "U.S. Self-Storage Industry Statistics." https://www.sparefoot.com/self-storage/news/1432-self-storage-industry-statistics/.

Harrison, Tish Warren. *Liturgy of the Ordinary: Sacred Practices in Everyday Life*. Downers Grove, IL: InterVarsity, 2016.

Hauerwas, Stanley. *Prayers Plainly Spoken*. Eugene, OR: Wipf and Stock, 2003.

Hellerman, Joseph. *When the Church Was a Family: Recapturing Jesus' Vision for Authentic Christian Community*. Nashville: B&H, 2009.

Hilbrand, Sonia, David A. Coall, Denis Gerstorf, and Ralph Hertwig. "Caregiving within and beyond the family is associated with lower mortality for the caregiver: A prospective study." *Journal of Evolution and Human Behavior* 38.3 (May 2017) 397–403.

Hendrix, John. *Shooting at the Stars: The Christmas Truce of 1914*. New York: Harry N. Abrams, 2014.

———. *The Faithful Spy: Dietrich Bonhoeffer and the Plot to Kill Hitler*. New York: Harry N. Abrams, 2018.

Hitchen, Danielle, and Jessica Blanchard. *Baby Believer Series*. Eugene, OR: Harvest House, 2018–2020.

Hrdy, Sarah Blaffer. *Mothers and Others: The Evolutionary Origins of Mutual Understanding*. Cambridge, MA: Harvard University Press, 2011.

Hunkin, Oliver. *Dangerous Journey: The Story of Pilgrim's Progress*. Grand Rapids: Eerdmans, 1985.

Kang, S. Steve, and Gary Parrett. *Teaching the Faith, Forming the Faithful*. Downers Grove, IL: InterVarsity, 2009.

King, Martin Luther, Jr. *I Have a Dream: Excerpts from Dr. Martin Luther King Jr.'s Speech*. Illustrated by Kadir Nelson. New York Schwartz & Wade, 2012.

Kohlberg, Lawrence. "The Development of Modes of Thinking and Choices in Years 10 to 16." PhD diss., University of Chicago, 1958.

Kornhaber, A., and K. L. Woodward. "The Grandparent/Grandchild Relationship: Family Resource in an Era of Voluntary Bonds." *Family Relations Journal* 34.3 (July, 1985) 343–52.

Lloyd-Jones, Sally. *The Jesus Storybook Bible: Every Story Whispers His Name*. Grand Rapids: ZonderKIDS, 2007.

Lock, S. "Number of McDonald's restaurants in North American from 2012 to 2019, by country." https://www.statista.com/statistics/256040/mcdonalds-restaurants-in-north-america/.

Lucado, Max, and Ron DiCianni. *Tell Me the Secrets: Treasures for Eternity*. Wheaton, IL: Crossway, 2015.

———. *Tell Me the Story: A Story for Eternity*. Wheaton, IL: Crossway, 2015.

Maimone, Melissa. Melissa Maimone blog October 29, 2013. https://www.melissamaimone.com/blog.

Miller, Lisa. *The Spiritual Child: The New Science on Parenting for Health and Lifelong Thriving*. UK: Picador, 2016.

Moorman, Sara M., and Jeffrey E. Stokes. "Solidarity in the Grandparent-Adult Grandchild Relationship and Trajectories of Depressive Symptoms." *The Gerontologist* 56.3 (June 2016) 408–20.

BIBLIOGRAPHY

Nouwen, Henri. *The Return of the Prodigal Son: A Story of Homecoming*. New York: Doubleday, 1994.

Okholm, Trevecca. *Kingdom Family: Re-Envisioning God's Plan for Marriage and Family*. Eugene, OR: Cascade, 2012.

———. "Reimagining the Role of Family in 21st Century Family Faith Practices." In *Bridging Theory and Practice in Children's Spirituality: New Directions for Education, Ministry, and Discipleship*, edited by Mimi L. Larson and Robert J. Keeley, 101–13. Grand Rapids: Zondervan, 2020.

Ortman, Jennifer M., Victoria A. Velkoff, and Howard Hogan. *An Aging Nation: The Older Population in the United States: Population Estimates and Projections*. Issued May 2014. P25-1140. U.S. Department of Commerce. Economics and Statistics Administration. Census.gov.

Parsley, Ross. *Messy Church: A Multigenerational Mission for God's Family*. Colorado Springs: David C. Cook, 2012.

Pfatteicher, Philip H. *Journey into the Heart of God: Living the Liturgical Year*. Oxford: Oxford University Press, 2013.

Pritchard, Sheila. "Digging Wells or Building Fences." Article sourced from *Radical Faith* website. (First published in *Reality* February/March, 1994.) https://shalomcarcoar.com/2017/02/12/digging-wells-or-building-fences/.

Ramsey, Becky. https://beckyramsey.info/.

Ramsey, Calvin Alexander, and Bettye Stroud. *Belle, the Last Mule at Gee's Bend: A Civil Rights Story*. Somerville, MA: Candlewick, 2016.

Ramsey, Calvin Alexander, Gwen Strauss, and Floyd Cooper. *Ruth and the Green Book*. Minneapolis: Carolrhoda, 2010.

Raschka, Chris. *Paul Writes (a Letter)*. Grand Rapids: Eerdmans, 2018.

Rice, Wayne. *Long Distance Grandparenting: Nurturing the Faith of Your Grandchildren When You Can't be There in Person*. Grand Rapids: Baker, 2019.

Roberto, John. *Re-Imagining Faith Formation for the 21st Century: Engaging All Ages and Generations*. Lifelong Faith Associates, 2015.

Rohr, Richard. *Falling Upward: A Spirituality for the Two Halves of Life*. San Francisco: Jossey-Bass, 2011.

Ruskin, Gary. "Why Children Whine: How Corporations Prey on our Children." *Mothering.com/articles/why-they-whine*. September 19, 2012.

Schoolman, Judith. "'The Nag Factor' Plays Role in What Parents Buy: Only 31 Percent of Parents Are Immune to Their Kids' Whining." *Toronto Star*, August 24, 1998.

Smalley, Gary, and John Trent. *The Blessing*. New York: Pocket, 1990.

Smith, Warren Cole. "C. S. Lewis, Madeleine L'Engle, and the Power of Storytelling." November 29, 2018. https://rabbitroom.com/2018/11/c-s-lewis-madeline-lengle-and-the-power-of-storytelling/.

Steinküler, Martin, and Barbara Nascimbeni. *Prayers for Young Children*. Grand Rapids: Eerdmans, 2018.

Stewart, Sonja. *Following Jesus*. Louisville: Geneva, 2000.

Taylor, Barbara Brown. *An Altar in the World: A Geography of Faith*. San Francisco: HarperOne, 2009.

Trafton, Jennifer, and Brett Helquist. *The Rise and Fall of Mount Majestic*. London: Puffin, 2011.

Turner, Robin. *Worship with Children*. https://www.worshipwithchildren.com/.

BIBLIOGRAPHY

Uhlenberg, Peter. "The Burden of Aging: A Theoretical Framework for Understanding the Shifting Balance of Caregiving and Care Receiving as Cohorts Age." *The Gerontologist* 36.6 (December 1996) 761–67.

Uhlenberg, P., and J. B. Kirby. "Grandparenthood Over Time: Historical and Demographic Trends." In *Handbook on Grandparenthood,* edited by M. E. Szinovacz, 23–39. Westport, CT: Greenwood, 1998.

Vittrup, Brigitte. "Exploring the Impact of Educational Television and Parent-Child Discussions on Children's Racial Attitudes." *Analyses of Social Issues and Public Policy* 10.1 (2010) 192–214.

Voskamp, Ann. *One Thousand Gifts: A Dare to Live Fully Right Where You Are.* Grand Rapids: Zondervan, 2011.

Wallace, Robin Knowles. *The Christian Year: A Guide for Worship and Preaching.* Nashville: Abingdon, 2011.

Waltke, Bruce. "The Way of Wisdom from the Book of Proverbs." Audiocassette. Vancouver, BC: Regent Audio, 2002.

Waters, Brent. *The Family in Christian Social and Political Thought.* New York: Oxford University Press, 2007.

Wilson, Carol S. *Keeping Sabbath with Young Children.* UK: Circle, 2010.

Wise, Cat. "What Happens When a Nursing Home and a Day Care Center Share a Roof?" *PBS Making the Grade.* May 10, 2016.

Woodruff, Paul. *Reverence: Renewing a Forgotten Virtue.* New York: Oxford University Press, 2014.

www.ingramcontent.com/pod-product-compliance
Lightning Source LLC
Chambersburg PA
CBHW031426150426
43191CB00006B/420